Global Development: Problems, Solutions, Strategy

RENEWALS 458-4574

DATE DUE

Series **Shifting Paradigms**

William Graham-Smith
CREATIVE LEAPS SHAPE THE WORLD
The History of the Future

Koenraad Kortmulder
PLAY AND EVOLUTION
Second Thoughts on the Behaviour of Animals

Frans Doorman
GLOBAL DEVELOPMENT: PROBLEMS, SOLUTIONS, STRATEGY
A Proposal for Socially Just, Ecologically Sustainable Growth

Frans Doorman

GLOBAL DEVELOPMENT: PROBLEMS, SOLUTIONS, STRATEGY

A Proposal for Socially Just, Ecologically Sustainable Growth

International Books

ISBN 90 5727 008 0
Keywords: Development, economy, environment

Desk Top Publishing: Hanneke Kossen
Cover design: Marjo Starink
Coverphoto: NASA
Printing: Haasbeek

International Books, Alexander Numankade 17, 3572 KP Utrecht, The Netherlands
tel +31 30 2731840, fax +31 30 2733614, e-mail i-books@antenna.nl

'That action is best,
which provides greatest happiness for the greatest numbers.'

Francis Hutcheson

TABLE OF CONTENTS

Part 2 Solutions

Part 3 Money

PROLOGUE

Never in history has mankind made such rapid progress as in the Twentieth century. In the rich nations, technological advances and forty years of peace have raised standards of living to unprecedented levels: never before have so many people lived so well, nor so long. Diseases that were lethal only decades ago have been eliminated, or can now be cured. The world's industries can produce an ever-larger array of increasingly complex goods for ever lower prices. People can travel to the most remote parts of the planet in a matter of days, and communicate all over the world within seconds. Economies are growing, and inflation is under control. In the rich nations, the most rampant forms of environmental pollution have been reduced significantly compared to twenty or thirty years ago. On the political front things have lightened up as with the fall of the totalitarian regimes of the former East Bloc, the threat of World War III and thereby, nuclear annihilation, has practically disappeared.

This is good news. Still, many people have doubts. Lower and middle wage earners find that jobs that only yesterday seemed secure, today are in danger. Many workers who manage to hold on to their position wonder why, in spite of continued economic growth and rising productivity, they have to work harder and harder whereas their purchasing power remains the same or in some cases, decreases. Those who lose their jobs are hard put to find new employment with similar pay and perks.

Simultaneously, poverty is growing in many poor countries—a category that today, includes most of the former East Bloc. Large sections of the population are unemployed or underemployed, while even those with a full time job often do not earn enough to feed, house and clothe themselves and their families adequately. Most of these people find it ever more difficult to carve out their stake in an increasingly efficient, competitive and demanding global economy. Their plight is worsened by the fact that in many nations, rich as well as poor, public education and health care are in decline. Thus,

the chances for the less well-off, and especially their children, to partake successfully in the economy are steadily reduced.

A look at the future gives more cause for concern. If current trends continue, fifty years from now a much larger global population will be competing for far fewer natural resources. Scarcity of oil, metals, fresh water and
agricultural land could raise the prices of many basic necessities, including
food. Pollution increasingly affects seas and even oceans, whereas disruptions
in the balance of the world's atmosphere could lead to heavier storms, more
severe droughts and flooding, and rising sea levels. Costly measures may be
needed to either prevent major disasters or repair the damage they will cause.
Poor nations will be unable to do so.

These problems are serious. Yet the development of new technology that
can resolve many of these problems continues. Many experts contend that
technical and economic progress will create the means needed to effectively
tackle these issues. So where do we stand? Is life going to get worse or better?
What situation will future generations find themselves in, and what should
we do to assure the best possible quality of life for all?

In this book I'll try to provide answers to these questions. My starting
point is that humanity should strive for a situation in which all people, all
over the world, can live in liberty and health, in a clean environment, with
sufficient land, water and other natural resources to ensure a decent
quality of life. The way to achieve this state is through *sustainable development*. The term 'development' indicates that getting from the present to
the desired situation is a gradual process. 'Sustainable' means that to get to
that state and maintain it, the world's resources will have to be used in
such a way that now and in the future, there will be enough for all. The
aim of sustainable development, then, is to ensure that all people of present
and future generations have equal access to all things required to ensure a
decent quality of life.

Quality of life has both a physical and a spiritual component. Physical
health requires an uncontaminated environment, clean drinking water, adequate food, shelter and sanitary conditions, and access to proper health care.
The spiritual component implies living in freedom: in a society in which
people are allowed to live their lives as they see fit, limited only by the right
of others to do the same. To live in freedom means having the liberty to make
choices. To make those in the best possible way, people should have unlimited access to knowledge and information. To use these optimally they
should, especially in the first years of their lives, receive all the attention, care

and education that is needed to fully develop their potential in body, mind and spirit.

This book analyses the obstacles to sustainable development, and suggest ways in which those obstacles can be overcome. Part 1 presents a broad overview of humanity's main economic, social and environmental problems, and discusses their causes and interrelationships. Part 2 offers solutions, in the form of set of measures aimed at setting society on the road to sustainable development. Part 3 discusses both conventional and unorthodox ways of financing the measures proposed in Part 2, and Part 4 presents a strategy for implementation by having people, worldwide, join forces in a single, global movement for change.

To analyze the world's problems, propose solutions, and present a strategy for sustainable development is, to say the least, ambitious. The reader may rightfully ask what brought me to attempt this undertaking, and what credentials I have to bring it to a proper ending.

Both my academic and my professional career have allowed me to confront the issues of global development firsthand. During the 1970s I studied sociology with a focus on developing nations at the Agricultural University of Wageningen, the Netherlands. The skills I learned in the systematic gathering of information and its interpretation through the critical use of relevant concepts and theories greatly helped me to develop the ideas put forward in this book. After my studies, I worked for fifteen years in development cooperation in Latin America and Africa, where I gained a first hand view of the daily struggle of people trying to provide themselves and their families with sustenance and a chance to improve their lives. Long and short term assignments in twelve different countries, and travel in various other ones, gave me both the bottom-up and the top-down viewpoints on the causes of Third World poverty. The combination of both perspectives made me reach the conclusion that many development models work for the fortunate few rather than for the unfortunate many, increasing, rather than alleviating, the misery of the poor.

My experience in the field led me—along with many colleagues—to question the established dogma's on the development of poor countries. It also brought me to examine more closely the predominant ideas on the advancement of the rich nations. In particular, I started to wonder about the inconsistencies between every day reality—as seen and talked about in one's own surroundings, read about in the newspapers, and seen on television—and the declarations of politicians, economists and other opinion leaders. Reality is, for example, that world-wide, over the past ten years, trade has become freer, taxes on the rich have been lowered, government budgets have been cut, and productivity (the amount of goods and services produced per worker) has increased. According to our political and economic pundits, all this should have led to increased wealth for all. Yet reality is different: the number of poor has grown, lower incomes have shrunk, and the expendable income of much of the middle class has either stagnated or declined.

Another question I pondered was why over the past two decades, in spite of strong economic growth and an enormous accumulation of wealth in the top layers of society, economists and politicians have been telling us there is not enough money for important goals such as improving education, protecting the environment or fighting poverty. Indeed, I began to ask myself how lack of *money*—which after all is a wholly artificial entity that in principle, can be created at will—can be an obstacle to any urgently needed measures.

The media provided few sensible answers to these questions. I found that as a rule natural scientists, such as ecologists, biologists and climatologists, limit themselves to describing what will happen if present trends continue, but offer little in terms of solutions. They leave that to politicians and economists, who either play down or negate society's problems, or proclaim that economic growth will solve them all. The discrepancies between their rhetoric and my own view on reality inspired me to use my knowledge, experience and powers of reasoning to analyze society's problems, search for solutions, and propose them to the reader in a coherent way.

Putting things on paper greatly helped to order and further develop my thoughts. It forced me to take a closer look at discrepancies in my observations, and brought to light inconsistencies in my reasoning. At the same time, I began to see that people too easily allow their own observations, ideas and arguments, however well-reasoned, to be discarded off-hand by those considered specialists. I found that especially economists have the tendency to put aside anything that does not fit their dogma's—and that unfortunately, non-economists, including scientists from other disciplines, let them get away with it. I hope, therefore, that if anything, this book will stimulate readers to develop their own thoughts and reasoning—taking account of, but not being bridled by, existing ideas and theories on how society works. Anyone with sufficient interest and a sound capacity for reasoning can do so, through the analysis of everyday observation and experience, a good newspaper, and the occasional reading of news magazines and broadly aimed scientific publications.

This book is based for an important part on information from the Dutch newspaper *de Volkskrant*, and from the news magazines *Newsweek* and *The Economist*. Additional information on the environment and on Third World poverty was derived from the annual editions of *State of the World*, the yearly Report on Progress towards a Sustainable Society published by the U.S. based World Watch Institute. Also, I made use of *The Earth Report 2*, edited by Edward Goldsmith and Nicholas Hildyard, the 1992 book *Beyond the limits* by Donella Meadows, Dennis Meadows and Jorgen Randers, and the 1993 edition of Paul Harrison's book *Inside the Third World: the anatomy of poverty*. My ideas on economics and money benefitted from two books by political economist Prof. John Kenneth Galbraith: the 1975 edition of his *Money: whence it came, where it went*, and the 1993 edition of his book *The Culture of Contentment*. Another valuable publication, pointed out to me by my publisher Jan van Arkel, was Richard Douthwaite's 1996 book *Short circuit: Strengthening Local Economies for security in an Unstable World*. Where relevant, the source of specific information and complete bibliographical data are given in footnotes.

I started this book in 1992 and have worked through three successive versions—each time, trying to make it more readable by limiting myself to the most important issues, and describing these as lucidly as possible. The result now lies before you. I hope it will stimulate the reader to critically analyze, as I did, what many of our mainstream politicians, economists, columnists and other opinion leaders claim to be universal truths. Even more, I hope it will help people to better understand what is happening in the world today and what should be done about it, as a basis for further action for sustainable development.

ACKNOWLEDGMENTS

Several people have commented on early drafts of this book: Richard Hawkins, Rob and Tineke Huizinga, and Alenka Verbole. Others have greatly improved the present version by pointing out weak spots and editing grammatical errors, among whom Carlos Escobar and especially, Ralph and Lynn Jackson stand out. My publisher, Jan van Arkel, and Jan Pen, Peter Pennartz, Leonardo Salazar, and André and Marc Verdegem also supplied valuable comments. In particular I would like to thank Jan for his willingness to take the risk of publishing this book—a gamble based much more on idealism than on business sense. I am also grateful to the staff of Jan van Arkel / International Books, in particular Trees Vulto, for their effort to turn the manuscript into the good-looking publication it has become. Finally, my most special thanks, and apologies, are due to my wife, Cristina, and my children Mark and Paula, who over the last few years have had to spend too much time without me.

Part 1

PROBLEMS

'We have not inherited the earth from our forefathers, but borrowed it from our children.'

Old Amerindian proverb

Chapter 1

THE ECONOMY

Wages, productivity and demand

People worry about their economic situation. They work harder and produce more, but don't see it in their paychecks. Whereas in the past they were fairly sure that, if they did a good job, they could stay with their employer for as long as they wanted, now they can be laid off at any moment. Before, it was often an employee's decision to leave a job, in exchange for a better one. Today, the initiative lies with employers: even when making record profits, companies lay off thousands of people. Only a handful manages to find new jobs with similar or better pay and benefits. The rest have to settle for lower salaries and fewer perks, or remains permanently unemployed.

This is a new phenomenon. From World War II up to the 1980s, periods of economic growth meant more and better paying jobs. In the 1980s, however, things changed. In 1994, the U.S. and European economies were well into an economic recovery. Yet in that same year, in the rich countries—North America, Europe and Japan—about 35 million people were registered as out of work. This figure did not include an estimated 15 million persons who had given up looking for jobs altogether, or worked less than they would have liked. Thus, in 1994, one out of every eight members of the work force could be considered as either unemployed or underemployed.[1]

By 1997, in spite of continued economic growth, these figures had not improved significantly. In fact, the number of officially unemployed had risen slightly, to a total of 36 million—about 7 1/2 per cent of the total work force.[2]

In Europe, with jobless rates topping 10%, the unemployment problem is greatest. The U.S. economy has been more successful in creating jobs: in 1995 and 1996, less than 6% of the work force was out of work; by 1997, the figure was down to 5%.[3] However, many of the new jobs are poorly paid, adding to an overall downward tendency in wages. In the 1980s, earnings in the lowest paid 10% of jobs fell by an average of more than 1% each year—

without accounting for inflation. Measurements of real income (earnings corrected for inflation) show that not only the lower, but also the middle class has suffered: in the 1980s the bottom 70% of U.S. income earners saw their purchasing power reduced by about 20%.[4]

In the 1990s, this trend has continued. In 1993, with the economy well into the recovery that followed the 1988-1991 recession, the income of the average American household declined by $312. Disposable income (that which remains after fixed costs such as taxes, mortgage payments, utilities, insurance, and school fees are subtracted) decreased even further as citizens were obliged to contribute more to the cost of education, health care, pension plans and other services and entitlements. For the lowest incomes, continuing government cutbacks in welfare and other social services have depressed living standards even further. In combination with the downward trend in wages this has led to an increase in the number of poor, from 32 million in 1993 to 39 million in 1995.[5]

Why is this happening? Why is it that the incomes of most people decrease, even though they work harder and produce more than ever before? Why don't economic growth and rapid technological development raise people's living standards?

It's not in line with economic theory. Economists claim that when productivity—the amount of goods and services produced per worker—goes up, so do wages. The above figures show this doesn't happen. And the reason is not that the economists' prescriptions are not being followed. Governments, so the recipe says, should promote economic growth by stimulating business. To do so regulations aimed at protecting workers, the environment and consumers have to be reduced, and taxes lowered. This, governments have done. Also, trade between countries should be promoted by making it easier to import and export products and capital. This stimulates growth by forcing companies to become more competitive, which raises efficiency and productivity. This has happened. But again, it has not led to higher wages. Still, economists advise more of the same medicine: even lower taxes and lesser regulation. That, so they argue, is the only way out of our problems.

It is not. What economists recommend and what governments are prone to do these days will, in the longer run, only make matters worse. Our fundamental problem is stagnating demand. Today, with real incomes declining and large scale lay-offs, the lower and middle income groups spend less on buying goods and services. Thus, consumer demand stagnates. That means that increased productivity does not translate into the same number of workers making more, but in fewer workers making the same amount of prod-uct. Simultaneously, competition between companies, which all want to sell as much as possible, becomes fiercer. This forces them to try even harder to raise efficiency and productivity—notably, by cutting costs. The result is more firings and a further decline in wages for those who remain. Unem-ployment rises, workers can spend even less, and demand shrinks further, stimulating even fiercer competition. And so on. In other words: our econ-omy is trapped in a vicious circle of rising productivity and stagnating or shrinking demand.

The outcome of this process can be observed in the sector where the gap between productivity and demand has grown widest: agriculture. Demand in this sector is fairly stable: people can eat only so much, and there are limits to the number of uses to which agricultural products can be put. Competition between farmers to satisfy this demand leads to increased efficiency and thus, to higher production. With demand stagnant, that leads to oversupply and consequently, lower product prices. That forces farmers to produce even more efficiently, which raises production even further. As a result, there is more oversupply, and prices drop even more. The less efficient producers are forced out of business, those remaining keep running the competitive rat race until they fall out of the treadmill themselves.

The result of this process is that today, in the rich countries, only a few percent of the work force is still employed in agriculture. In the U.S. and Northern Europe, one farmer produces enough to feed up to 40 to 50 non-agricultural families. That means farmers make up only some 2% of the working population—compared to close to 50% a century or so ago. Even so, many economists consider the agricultural sector as inefficient. Especially in Europe and Japan there are still large numbers of relatively small farmers who, according to economic criteria, should have gone out of business long ago. Out of love for the trade, and because they see no alternative, they con-tinue to work long hours for a minimal income. Subsidies, mostly in the form of artificially high prices, help them survive. If market forces were given free reign, most of this group would be forced out of business in a matter of years. Even with subsidies, the number of farmers is likely to go down to 1% or less of the working population in the not too distant future. In other words, in modern agriculture, productivity has been raised to such levels that only 1% of the working population can satisfy all demand.

Will the same happen in the industrial and service sectors? Not to the same extent. Demand for industrial goods and services is more flexible than that for agricultural products: companies always seem to be able to come up with new things we would like to have or do. Yet there are limits to the amount of products consumers can handle—and there are indications that the saturation point is close. Because of the enormous variety of products already on the market, producers are finding it increasingly difficult to attract consumers' attention to new ones. Marketing experts have even coined a phrase for this phenomenon: 'product clutter'.

So, as far as consumers are concerned, there are two factors that keep demand from keeping up with productivity growth. One is absorption capacity, the other stagnating incomes. But consumers are not the only demand category that is falling behind: government also has less to spend. Starting in the 1970s, governments have built up huge debts. Now, budgets are burdened by the interest that has to be paid over these debts, and by their payment. Moreover, there is a worldwide drive to reduce or eliminate budget deficits, and continuing pressure to lower taxes. Finally, in countries with high unemployment and extensive social security systems, unemployment benefits swallow up ever larger proportions of national budgets. All this leaves governments precious little funds for the purchase of goods and services. In the u.s., for example, investment in infrastructure has been halved since the 1970s. Thus, decreasing demand from the government combines with slack consumer demand to depress overall demand in the economy.

As long as overall demand keeps stagnating or even declining, it is no more than logical to expect that in industry and services, a development comparable to that in the agricultural sector will take place. That would mean that within a few decades, a work force making up only a minor percentage of the population would be able to satisfy all the demand the economy would generate. Fortunately, that phase is still far off. In fact, as economists will be quick to point out, up till now demand has fairly well kept its own. They use this as an argument to support the theory that rising productivity leads to new wealth and therefore, increased demand, jobs, and economic growth. The facts appear to support them: after all, the phenomenon of stagnating middle and lower incomes dates back to the early 1980s, yet the mid-1990s still showed robust economic growth. Where does that leave the theory of the growing gap between productivity and demand?

The answer is that the theory hasn't really been tested yet—but will be in the near future. Although the stagnation of lower and middle incomes began in the 1980s, it has up to now not led to a significant decline in overall demand. One reason for this is deficit financing: over the last decade people and governments have lent money to make up for the shortage of disposable income. Thus both consumer and government demand were sustained. Today, however, with people and governments more indebted than ever before in history, this strategy has run its course. Both consumers and governments must reduce their debts and therefore, their spending.

Another reason why so far demand has kept up is that slack consumer demand has been compensated for by heavy investment in capital goods: the machinery and other equipment business needs to make its products. As we've seen, fierce competition has led to a strong drive to increase efficiency and productivity. To do so, producers invest in new technology. Thus, the competitive rat race has been a boon for the producers of capital goods that incorporate such technology. Moreover, growth markets in especially Asia and to a lesser extent, Latin America have contributed to strong sales in capital goods. Yet in the end, these capital goods will have to be paid for by the sale of products to consumers. With stagnating or falling demand, that is going to be increasingly difficult. Therefore, in the near future, demand for capital goods is also likely to diminish.

In conclusion, then, the growing gap between productivity and demand will lead to a vicious circle of declining real wages and growing unemployment. That it hasn't up till now is because consumer demand has been sustained by deficit spending, and because demand for capital goods has been strong. As these strategies run their course, the effects of stagnating demand and growing productivity will make themselves felt with a vengeance.

Wealth concentration and speculation

Now, let's go back to the premise of economists that as efficiency and productivity increase, more wealth is created. This wealth, so they argue, will either be consumed or invested in the production of goods and services. Both will create demand for consumer goods, services and capital goods, and thus, jobs.

This is partly true. However, because of the above described process, the wealth created is less than it should be. Stagnating incomes make for lesser demand for consumer goods, and fierce competition depresses profit margins. As a result, there is less room for investment. Moreover, in recent years another limiting factor has presented itself. It is that more and more, the wealth created by rising productivity is no longer used for consumption or investment, but for speculation: the trade in financial securities, especially stocks, or in currencies, in the hope of making a quick, windfall profit.

As we've seen, the wealth created by rising productivity does not end up with the lower and middle income groups. Instead, most of it goes to a relatively small group of people: management, owners and shareholders. Especially managers have, over the last decade, been as skillful in raising their own salaries as they have been in cutting jobs. In addition to huge raises in gross income, the rich have also benefitted from tax cuts. This has led to an enormous concentration of wealth: in the u.s., by 1993, the richest one-half percent of the population owned 31% of the nation's wealth, with the next one-half owning another 9.[6]

The rich, of course, are experts in throwing money around. Yet today they have so much of it that despite these considerable skills they are able to spend only a fraction of what they earn. Giving away more than the token contributions to charities is, of course, not an option. Therefore, what they cannot spend and do not want to give away they reinvest—to try to gain even more wealth.

Here, however, they run up against the already discussed problem of stagnating demand. Lesser spending by lower and middle income consumers and the government leads to reduced opportunities for business. That translates into lesser returns on investment in the productive sector of the economy, where goods and services are produced. Luckily, there is a way out. Thanks to the worldwide opening up of capital markets, an international financial circuit has formed with an almost limitless capacity to absorb capital. The rich can sluice their money into this market by purchasing internationally traded securities, such as stocks and bonds. In the last few years, the amount of money doing the rounds in this international financial circuit has grown enormously. Consider: from 1990 to 1993, in just three years, the capital involved almost tripled, to $3 trillion.[7]

Economists don't distinguish between investment in the productive sector of the economy and buying internationally traded stocks. They'll point out that the very purpose of issuing stock is to generate capital for investment. They are right—in theory. In practice, however, things work out differently. If the money poured in stocks would really be invested in production, it would be tied up in capital goods. But it isn't: the money circulating in the international financial circuit isn't tied to anything. It hovers over the real, physical economy, and is, at any given moment, moved around the globe at lightning speed, through a few keystrokes on the computers operated by money managers. As indeed happens: each day, about one trillion dollars in securities and currencies is traded. Only about 1% of this volume is linked to the actual trade in goods and services.[8] The other 99% involves transactions aimed at (quick) capital gains, that is, speculation.

An important part of the wealth created through rising productivity, then, no longer leads to new jobs, as it did in the past, but disappears into the international financial circuit. But the failure to create jobs is not the only problem. Speculation leads, almost by definition, to a financial crash. Such crashes are, as a rule, followed by an economic crisis. The danger of this happening is increased as the amount of speculative capital grows faster. If the latter is not paired with rapid growth in the supply of stocks, the price of the latter will be driven up. That's exactly what is happening today. Take Wall Street, the biggest financial market: in ten years (from mid-June 1985 to mid-June 1995), the value of the most traded stocks (as shown by the Dow Jones index) rose by 246%, from 1298 to 4496 points. By early 1997, the Dow Jones had risen to over 7000, by mid 1998, to 8000. Yet in that same period, the economy expanded by only some 30%.[9]

These figures point to a situation in which the price of stocks has little to do with the actual value of companies. The latter is determined by their present and projected turn-over, competitiveness, assets, and profits. Although all these factors may have improved considerably over the past decade, they are unlikely to have increased, on the average, six-fold. Another indicator of the speculative character of the recent rise in prices is the reason for buying stock. Whereas in the past, people bought stocks largely for the dividends (the part of the company's yearly profits paid to shareholders), today this motive has become much less important: stocks are bought primarily because buyers expect their value to rise, with dividends being considered only of secondary importance.

With more and more capital flowing into the financial markets, prices of stocks are likely to go up even more. At a certain moment, even money managers will realize that the value for which they are traded is way beyond their real value. A minor event, such as disappointing profits or a loss posted by a major company will trigger a panic, and stocks will crash. That will result in an economic recession and possibly, a depression. As a result, many small and medium sized businesses will fail and workers will lose their jobs. Thus, the price for speculation is paid by the lower and middle income groups. In fact, this group is likely to be hit twice, since as taxpayers they'll have to shoulder most of the burden of repairing the financial system. A foretaste of what that can involve was given in the 1980s' Savings and Loans affair in the u.s., and the 1990s' banking scandal in Japan. In both cases, failed banks had to be bailed out with taxpayer money, at a total cost of tens of billions of dollars.

Tax cuts

As said, the above problems are due for an important part to the concentration of wealth among the top layers of society. This concentration has been stimulated by the tax cuts that were initiated in the 1980s. Nevertheless, tax cuts remain a popular item on the political agenda. Yet the way they are carried out implies only minor gains for the lower and middle income groups: most of the wealth of the across-the-board tax cuts that economists and politicians advocate end up with the rich. Thus, it has been estimated that due to the u.s. tax cuts of the 1980s, some 70% of the economic growth of that decade ended up with the richest 1% of the population.[10]

Despite the enormous wealth that already has come their way, the rich are not satisfied: they demand even bigger tax cuts. A good example is the so-called flat tax. This is presented as an alternative to current income tax systems, in which higher incomes pay a higher percentage in taxes than lower incomes. With a flat tax, everybody pays the same percentage over his or her income—independently of how much is earned.

Let's look at the consequences of instituting a 20% flat tax in an economy where the tax rate is 20% over the first $30,000 of income, 30% on everything between $30,000 and $100,000, and 40% for everything over $100,000. For those earning $30,000 or less, a 20% flat tax doesn't make any difference: they still have to pay 20% of their income in taxes. People making $40,000 will pay 10% less tax over everything they make over $30,000: instead of paying $3000, they only have to pay $2000. Savings: $1000. People making $100,000 benefit considerably more: they save 10% over $70,000, or $7000. This pales, however, in comparison with the savings for the very rich: say, people making $1 million. In addition to the $7000 gained over the first $100,000 of their income, they save 20% over $900,000, that's $180,000 (Table 1). All in all, their extra benefits amount to $187,000—187 times as much as those of the average income earner who makes $40,000 a year, and more than 25 times as much as the upper middle class earner making $100,000.

TABLE I   *The benefits of the introduction of a flat tax for different income groups*

Income	$30,000	$40,000	$100,000	$1,000,000
Taxes due under a progressive tax system:				
20% over first $30,000	6,000	6,000	6,000	6,000
30% over $30,000 to $100,000 bracket	–	3,000	21,000	21,000
40% over earnings over $100,000	–	–	–	360,000
Total	6,000	9,000	27,000	387,000
Taxes due under flat tax system:				
20% over all income	6,000	8,000	20,000	200,000
Net gains	–	1,000	7,000	187,000

Small wonder, then, that the rich and those who represent them propose lower income taxes, a flat income tax, or even no income tax at all. What's surprising is that so many people with middle and lower incomes don't realize the consequences of supporting such proposals. Sure, they may gain a couple of hundred, or even a few thousand dollars in extra after-tax income. But tax cuts have to be paid for by raising other taxes, or through budget cuts. Either way, what is given by one hand is taken away with the other. Budget cuts imply there will be less money for education, health care, law enforcement, scientific research, public transport, environmental protection, cultural activities, open-air recreation, social security, care for the aged, and infrastructure such as roads, bridges, airports, and railways. Some of these cuts will affect longer term economic prospects, others will lead to more expensive or a deteriorating level of services. The latter may bring people who can afford it to look for similar services in the private sector—at, no doubt, a considerably higher cost. Even for upper middle incomes, this extra cost is likely to be much higher than the savings in taxes. All in all, then, the benefits of a flat tax are likely to be negative for the large majority of taxpayers: the only group that will really benefit is the rich.

Less tax income may also mean the government has to borrow to cover its expenses—as happened in the 1980s. The lenders will be the same rich who benefit from the tax cuts. Now there's a sweet deal. First, the government—and thus, taxpayers, most of whom are lower and middle income—gives money to the rich. Then, the same government has to borrow it back at a stiff interest rate. The ensuing debts, increased with compound interest, will have to be paid by those same middle and lower income taxpayers. Thus, the less well-off are duped into subsidizing the rich on a permanent basis.

Of course the rich, supported by most economists, say that it is in everybody's interest to lower their taxes. Less taxes, so they claim, will leave them more money to invest, and investment creates new and better paying jobs. But as we've already seen, this doesn't hold true. Instead of being invested in production, most of the money disappears in the international financial markets, where it is used primarily for speculation. This only creates employment for the small group of bankers and the other financial experts who manage these enormous money supplies. And note: these are the same bankers and experts who, in the 1980s, promoted the speculation that caused stock markets to crash, and who through reckless lending caused the already mentioned financial mess in the U.S. and Japan. Now, this same group pushes their clients to engage in speculation—just as they did in the 1980s, by promising that in the long run, the value of stocks will rise by 10% or more each year—in economies where economic growth is projected to grow by, at the most, 2 to 3%.

So thanks to our economists, bankers and other financial specialists, more financial crises are ahead. And, just as in the past, the middle class taxpayer and consumer will pay the bill: tax money will be used to bail out failed banks; the recession that will follow the crash will cause companies to fail and workers to lose their jobs. As in the past, banks will try to recover their losses by tempting people to buy on credit, so they can charge interest on loans and credit cards. Once more, the middle and lower income groups will pay the bills of the rich, and of those who manage their wealth. For the rich, of course, it's the perfect set-up. If speculation goes well, they receive the benefits. When things go wrong—as they always do at some point—taxpayers and consumers will pay most of the price.

Globalization

We've seen how, due to the growing gap between productivity and demand, fewer and fewer people can satisfy the demand for goods and services. That causes unemployment and brings down wages. To this can be added that in the rich countries, business is more and more inclined to move production to low wage countries. As transport and communications improve and obstacles to the free flow of goods and capital across borders disappear, transnationally operating companies can easily move production to the countries where conditions are best for them. In the last twenty or so years, that has already happened for goods which are simple to produce, such as clothes, shoes and toys. Today, most of these products are made in poor countries, where wages are twenty to forty times as low as in the rich nations. Increasingly, more complex goods are also produced in low wage countries, especially in East Asia.

Economists say that's good. Poor people in poor countries need these jobs, so it is said. According to economic theory, free trade causes each country to produce what it produces best. The rich countries, with a highly skilled work force and a lot of capital and technology, should manufacture complicated, expensive goods—such as machinery. Poor countries, with cheap labor and less investment capital, should make cheaper, easier to produce commodities such as clothes, toys and simple consumer electronics. Thus, everybody will benefit.

This is one of the most widely accepted theories in economics. It was developed, though, in the nineteenth century, in a time when companies did not move production from one country to another. Today, the ability of companies from rich nations to move production to low wage countries puts a whole new perspective on things. By moving machinery and highly skilled personnel, they can produce the same things as in their home country, but at a much lower cost. Moreover, several low wage countries have increasingly sophisticated work forces which, in comparison with similar personnel in the rich countries, cost next to nothing. India, for example, has a small army of software engineers, who can be hired for only one twelfth of what similarly skilled workers cost in the rich nations.[11] Small wonder, then, that more and more sophisticated production moves south. Thus, several major u.s. and European airlines and insurance companies have already moved their administration to India.

This spells big problems for workers, even higher skilled ones, in the rich countries. Economic logic may dictate that business in the rich countries should concentrate on high technology products that less developed countries cannot make. Yet once such products have been developed, there is no reason why production shouldn't be moved to a low wage country with highly skilled workers such as India—or, for example, Pakistan, Brazil, Thailand

and possibly, China. Imagine an American computer chip maker moving its production to India. Within a few years, it might even move its engineering section there. If many high tech companies do so—and there is no reason why they shouldn't—there would be little left to produce in the rich countries.

The point is this. Up to now, the move of production to low wage countries has hurt mostly low skilled workers. Soon, it will also hit the higher skilled workers that make up the u.s. and European middle class. Yesterday, textile workers, today, bookkeepers, tomorrow, software engineers. As middle and higher level jobs move to low wage countries, the middle class of the rich countries will come to face the same problems as the lesser skilled, lower income groups do today. This will come on top of the already considerable job losses with companies that 'downsize' and replace workers with ever more advanced machinery.

The position of labor

The above described processes—technological development, the gap between productivity and demand, and competition from poor countries—have combined to gradually erode the position of workers worldwide. Before, business was still closely tied to a specific country. That meant that in that country, employers needed workers as much as workers needed employers. This was especially so in times of economic expansion, when there was a lot of demand for labor. It led to a strong position for workers, which helped them acquire a wide range of rights: minimum wages, rules on worker safety, maximum working hours, unemployment benefits, the right to strike, health insurance, the right to vacation. The growing strength of trade unions also enabled workers to obtain regular pay raises and other benefits. In labor conflicts, employers were forced to give in at least partly to the demands of workers. There was no other course: they could not move away and set up shop in another country, with more 'employer friendly' conditions.

Today, many can. This option, and high unemployment, has led to a much weaker position of workers versus employers. The only group still holding a position of power is a salaried elite of highly trained engineers, designers, managers, researchers and consultants, whose skills are in great demand. As production becomes more complex, demand for them keeps growing, giving them a strong position versus employers. The need for their skills guarantees high salaries and all sorts of perks. On the other hand, because their number is relatively small, employers can fairly easily transfer them to another country to work there.

Thus, there is a new division among workers. On the one hand, there is the group of highly skilled, mobile people; on the other, the mass of lesser skilled blue and white collar workers. Today, the latter can be found in rich as well as in many poor countries, which makes them interchangeable. Without bargaining power, there is little they can do to obtain wage raises or other benefits. On the other hand, the rat race of competition fuelled by the gap between productivity and demand forces employers to cut production costs. Both tendencies contribute to people getting fired and wages lowered.

So what will the future bring? In the rich countries, workers will have no choice but to accept further cuts in wages and fewer perks. Yet in spite of this, unemployment will increase as production is moved to low wage countries, people are replaced by machinery, and stagnating demand makes for fewer business opportunities. A few poor countries will benefit from the move of production from high to low wage countries. It will bring jobs and better pay: transnational companies often pay better than local business. But in huge countries like India, Brazil, Indonesia and China, only a fairly small group of workers will benefit, and overall wage levels will remain low. They will have to: if wages rise too much, business can move to another country, where workers are paid even less. Or, as in the rich countries, workers will be replaced by machinery.

Chapter II

DESTITUTE POVERTY

Poverty in the rich nations

In Chapter I we've seen how the ranks of the poor are growing in the rich nations. This poverty is, to a certain extent, relative: people are poor compared to the rest of the population. Yet most poor families and individuals are still able to feed, dress, and shelter in ways that meet minimum standards. What they lack is the income needed to maintain a generally accepted standard of living. Every penny has to be turned twice before being spent, and goods and services that others take for granted are unaffordable. The poor depend on the lowest quality food and clothing and cannot afford to own their own home. There's no going places: vacationing is out of the question, restaurants and theaters are substituted for by television sets and another meal at home. At best, there is the occasional video rental and a visit to a fast food joint. Membership in sports clubs or other organizations is also too expensive, as are such extravagances as ballet or music lessons for the children. Life becomes a dreary treadmill of routine actions, in a depressing environment, without a possibility of even temporary escape.

Perhaps hardest to bear is that the prospects for permanent escape are diminishing also. In the past, poverty was accompanied by the hope that through hard work, people could improve their situation and escape from poverty. Even if they themselves could not, people had high hopes that their children would rise on the socio-economic ladder—as indeed, many did. Especially after World War II, the situation of the poor improved because the youngest generation had access to well-functioning public education systems. That and an expanding job market gave ample opportunities for advancement. Even if people stayed in relatively lowly jobs, their situation improved through the steady wage increases gained by powerful labor unions and increasing productivity.

Today, as we've seen, things are different. At the lower end of the job market, real wages are in decline. We've already seen how in the u.s., in the 1980s, earnings in the lowest paid 10% of jobs fell by an average of more than 1% each year. At the same time, the number of people living in poverty rose to more than 39 million—up 7 million from 1989. In Europe also, wages at the lower end of the scale are sliding. In Britain, the poorest 20% of the population lost close to $300 in annual expendable income between 1979 and 1989. Applying European Community poverty standards, Britain saw its number of working poor rise from 38% in 1979 to 47% in 1991.[1]

Weakened labor unions, the move of lowly skilled jobs to poor countries, and the loss of jobs and pressure on wages resulting from fierce international competition offer little hope for improvement. Worse, cutbacks in government expenditure reduce the chances of poor children to break the circle of poverty. With public education in decline and private schools out of reach, poor families find it increasingly difficult to provide their children with a good quality education. The overall lack of prospects has contributed importantly to social problems such as crime, alcohol and drug abuse, and family break-ups.

And the prospects? Most economists advise and politicians administer more of the same medicine. They advocate the abolishment of minimum wages. They recommend to let the market do its work. In a situation where the demand for lowly skilled jobs exceeds supply, that means the price of labor and therefore, wages, will diminish even further. They advocate free trade and the free flow of investment capital, which brings companies to move production to low wage countries. They hail the relentless drive for efficiency that brings companies to cut their work force while increasing the workload of those that remain. They recommend to lower taxes. That, unavoidably, will lead to the further decline of public services—including education and job training programs. It will also lead to lesser public investment and therefore, fewer jobs in sectors like construction which, traditionally, employ large numbers of relatively lowly skilled workers. In conclusion: neither recent economic developments nor mainstream political thought, including ideas on which way the economy and society should go, offer much hope for the future.

Destitute poverty

In the rich countries, poverty is defined as lacking the income needed to sustain an adequate living standard. Poverty is therefore relative. In the poor countries, poverty is absolute. People are so desperately poor that their lives are a daily struggle for survival. They lack the food, clothing and housing they need to subsist in a reasonable state of health. In a 1992 study, the United Nations estimated that some 700 million people—more than twice the population of the u.s.—are so poor they don't have enough to eat. Another 300 million people can only afford food of such poor quality that their diet lacks the necessary proteins, minerals and vitamins. This means that one billion persons, one-fifth of the world population, are, to use the official term, malnourished.[2]

Poverty is, of course, closely related to income. In 1992 the World Bank, one of the most prestigious institutions involved in international development, defined a 'poverty line' of $370 per year per person: about $1 a day.[3] Using this measure, it estimated that in 1990, there were 1.13 billion poor people: almost one third of the population of the developing world. Since then, the number has risen. In 1997, the United Nations Development Program (UNDP) estimated that 1.3 billion people were living below the poverty line. This figure did not include the growing number of poor in the former East Bloc, particularly in the former Soviet Union. In 1997, the poverty line for this region was put at u.s. $4 a day, with an estimated 120 million people, about a third of the population, living below it.[4]

Another indicator of absolute poverty is child mortality: the percentage of deaths of infants under the age of five. According to 1994 World Bank figures, child mortality rates among the poorest 600 million people approach 50%. An important cause of high child mortality is disease caused by contaminated drinking water—a problem which affects, according to UNDP estimates of 1997, well over a billion people. The same source indicates that in the poor countries nearly a billion people do not know how to read and write, and that 840 million go hungry.

To be sure, since the early 1960s some progress has been made in the fight against poverty. The United Nations Development Program (UNDP) notes, in its 1992 Human Development Report, that in the 1960-1990 period the average life expectancy in the developing countries increased by 17 years, from 46 to 63. Also, progress was made with regard to literacy, calorie intake, the reduction of child mortality and access to safe drinking water. This progress, however, was achieved largely in the 1960s and 1970s. In the 1980s, the upward trend was halted and in some cases reversed. In some countries, especially in Africa, life expectancies, access to drinking water and literacy have declined, while child mortality is on the rise again. Measured by income, the number of poor appears to be rising in every world region except South-East Asia and the Pacific.[5]

Poverty hits especially hard at women and children. Children are much more vulnerable to diseases caused by malnutrition and unclean drinking water than adults. Moreover, in many poor countries women and girls are worse off than males. Of the 1.1 billion of people living below the poverty line, the World Bank estimates that 70% are women. They have to work harder than men: in addition to child care and housekeeping, they also grow and process food. Simple tasks can take up huge amounts of time: many rural women have to walk for hours to fetch firewood or drinking water. What makes things worse is that many women are on their own: in one third to one fourth of the world's households, they are the sole breadwinners. In another one fourth, women contribute at least 50% of household income.[6]

Yet in spite of their heavy work load, women and girls eat less and have less to spend than men. In some cultures, most food and income go to the male family members, even though the needs of pregnant women and small children are greater. For Bangla Desh and Pakistan it has been estimated that as a result of this deprivation, the number of female deaths is one million higher than that of male deaths.

The growing gap

The presence of large groups of poor people is one of the main factors distinguishing rich from poor countries, and contributes to a huge gap in per capita incomes. In the 1993 World Bank Atlas, the average per capita income of the richest country in the world, Switzerland, is given as $36,410: 455 times as high as that of the poorest nation, Mozambique, at $80. The 2,83 billion people living in the poorest countries, 53% of the world's population, earned only 4.4% of the world's income. On the other hand, the 850 million living in the richest nations, making up 16% of humanity, were good for 78% of global wealth.[7]

In the 1950s and 60s there was widespread expectation that the gap between rich and poor countries would close. Development aid from the rich countries would help generate the growth and development that would allow the poor to catch up with the rich. If supplied with the needed capital and know-how, so it was argued, the economies of the poor countries would 'take off'. In time, the poor nations were expected to reach the same standard of living as the rich nations.

In spite of a few success stories, however, the overall gap between rich and poor has only increased, and continues to do so. In 1960, the poorest 20% of the world's people had a 2.3% stake in global income. In 1991, their share had shrunk to 1.4%, and in 1996, to 1.1%. The ratio of the income of the top 20% to that of the poorest 20% rose from 30 to 1 in 1960 to 61 to 1 in 1991— and a startling 78 to 1 in 1994.[8]

A prime characteristic of developing countries is that income disparities are much more marked than in the developed nations. Take Brazil. The richest 1% of its 150 million inhabitants gains 20% of the national income, the next 4% is good for another 20%. At the other end of the scale, some 100 million people, over 60% of the population, live in poverty. Most of these people are permanently malnourished; about 40 million go to bed hungry every night. Among them are 8 million homeless children who survive, if at all, through begging, prostitution and petty crime. Inequality is also reflected in land ownership: the top 2% of land owners possess 57% percent of all arable land, whereas half of all agricultural families don't own any.[9]

India is another example of a large poor nation with extreme inequality. Although it has its own nuclear weapons and space program, the Indian Council of Applied Economic Research estimates that out of a total population of 950 million, only some 245 million people enjoy a reasonable standard of living. Almost as large a number of people, 222 million, is classified as absolute poor; about 435 million live just above the poverty line.[10]

Most of the Indian poor live in the countryside; of the total rural population of 600 million, half is estimated to be chronically malnourished. Child labor is rampant: estimates from the South Asian Coalition against Child Slavery hold that as many as 50 million children, from 4 to 16 years old, are involved. They work up to 16 hours a day, seven days a week, for little or no wages. Abuse is widespread, but only the most extreme cases get publicity. That happened in October 1994, when the case of a 15 year old boy, burned alive by his employer for asking for a few days' rest, made the international press.

Causes of poverty

Let's begin by doing away with two fallacies. The first is, that poverty has a cultural cause, which is a nice way of saying that people are poor because they're lazy. It is true that different cultures value the drive to make money differently. But not even in those cultures or groups where property is valued least do people suffer from hunger and illness because they prefer being hungry or ill over working.

The second fallacy is that there are not enough resources in the world to provide for all of humanity. That is—not yet—the case. At world level, enough food is produced to provide the entire world population with an adequate diet. Also, it is technically and economically possible to provide all people with basic health care, adequate quality drinking water and other basic services. Absolute poverty is, therefore, a question of distribution rather than production. Resources and wealth are distributed unequally, both between and within countries.

Differences in the wealth of nations is sometimes attributed to the possession of natural resources. Certainly, the possession of minerals like oil can make a difference. But natural resources are neither a precondition nor a guarantee for wealth. The country with the second most powerful economy in the world, Japan, has very few of them. The same goes for the four countries that over the last few decades have developed most rapidly: Singapore, Taiwan, Hong Kong and Korea. On the other hand, countries like Zaire, Angola and Iraq, all replete with natural riches, are in dire straits. So are the economies, and large parts of the population of Mexico, Venezuela and Nigeria, countries with abundant oil supplies.

An important difference between countries such as Japan and Zaire is the presence of technical and managerial skills. These are essential for developing an advanced economy and for running a modern nation state. In the rich nations such skills are more prevalent than in the poor countries. In economic life, they are used to produce high value goods and services. The use of advanced technology leads to high productivity, and wages to match it. That is one of the reasons why in rich countries workers earn much higher wages than in poor nations.

Having the skills to develop and apply modern technology allows countries to produce a wide range of goods and services. Also, they can rapidly adapt to economic change. The capacity of poor countries to do so is much less. The least developed countries often depend solely on the export of raw materials: minerals or agricultural products. Sometimes, only one or two products have to earn the foreign exchange needed for such imports as machinery, chemicals and medicines. Over the last decades, however, the prices of most raw materials have plummeted. This has been due to decreasing demand, increasing supply, or both. Yet at the same time, the prices of imports have risen. This has been called the 'worsening terms of trade': the poor countries have to supply more and more of their traditional exports to pay for the same amount of imports.

Another cause of poverty is, obviously, low wage levels. Partly, these are due to low productivity. Yet as we've seen previously, there are many cases where in poor countries, productivity comparable to that in the rich nations earns people only a fraction of the wages paid there. This is, of course, exactly why many companies move production to low wage countries.

The problem for workers in poor countries is that they have little or no bargaining power. Workers that go on strike or protest low wages in other ways can be fired at will: there is a legion of unemployed to take their place. Trade unions, if they exist at all, are often suppressed, sometimes brutally. Also, there are the limitations imposed by the internationalization of the economy. If wages rise too much or workers become too troublesome, business can set up shop in another country, where conditions are more favorable.

Another factor that perpetuates poverty is protectionism from the rich nations. Although the latter pay lip service to free trade, they use a wide variety of measures, such as import quota or tariffs, to protect their producers from cheap imports. This is especially so for agricultural products. Moreover, price supports for producers in the rich countries lead to large scale overproduction. This is dumped on world markets, causing prices to fall. Also, subsidized exports from rich countries hurt producers in poor countries, who are neither protected nor subsidized by their governments. For example, in the early 1990s cattle farmers in Western Africa were battered by beef from the European community, which was sold at only a fraction of the price West European consumers had to pay. Similarly, in the 1980s and early 1990s small corn producers in Latin America were hard hit by cheap corn from the U.S.—which, ironically, was provided as aid.

The debt problem

Perhaps the single biggest cause of continuing poverty in the developing countries is the debt problem. It has its origins in the 1970s, when international financial institutions such as the World Bank and the International Monetary Fund (IMF), private banks and the governments of rich nations freely lent to the governments of poor countries. Loads of money were pumped into setting up huge industrial enterprises and developing economic infrastructure such as dams, irrigation works, roads, harbors, and railways. Unfortunately, a lot of these projects had more negative than positive effects. Many were poorly conceived, caused great environmental damage, and never led to the economic growth the planners had predicted.[11] Others were badly managed, often by corrupt officials. Even the few projects that did yield the expected increase in production earned less money than originally projected, because of the above mentioned worsening terms of trade.

Loans were also used for non-economic purposes. Supporters of the ruling political parties were given cushy jobs in the civil service, leading to rapidly expanding state bureaucracies. The support of urban middle class voters was bought by providing public housing and generous pension plans for government employees. Also, city people were kept content by subsidies on foodstuffs, medicine, petrol and public transport.

The actual use made of the loans, then, only rarely yielded enough money to pay them back. Moreover, even if projects were successful, little of the newly created wealth became available to pay back the loans. The taxes and user fees that had to be levied to do so were kept low to keep people happy. Tax collection was—and continues to be—extremely inefficient. Especially the wealthy individuals and businesses who benefitted most from development projects proved to be masters at tax evasion.

In 1982 all this, in combination with rapidly rising interest rates, led to the so-called debt crisis. Several major debtors, among them Mexico, were no longer able to pay the interest on their loans, let alone pay back the principal. If debtors can't pay their debts, banks get into trouble. A worldwide banking crisis was avoided, however, when under the leadership of the IMF and the World Bank, the debts were 'restructured'. Basically, this amounted to paying off old loans with new ones. Thus, repayment of the debts and the accumulated interest was postponed, and several major banks were saved.

But the debt problem is far from resolved. Since the crisis of 1982, the debt load of the developing countries has only increased. At the end of 1994, the total sum owned stood at $1945 billion, more than twice as high as the $850 billion due in 1982.[12,13] In 1996, the amount had risen to $2177 billion, up $112 billion, that's over 5%, from 1995.[14] This in spite of the fact that between 1982 and 1993, the developing countries paid about $2 trillion in interest and principal to their creditors: private banks and the governments of the rich nations, and the international financial institutions controlled by them. By 1992, payment on interest and principal was taking up an average of 40% of the poor nations' budgets.[15]

The above means that as things are going, the poor countries will remain permanently indebted. They will pay enough to stay financially afloat and remain eligible for new loans, but won't be able to pay off their debts. For the banks, this situation is favorable: returns on their capital, in the form of interest payments, keep flowing in. They will continue to do so as long as old loans are replaced by new ones, keeping the poor countries in a permanent state of financial dependency.

Those who suffer most from this dependency are the middle and lower income groups and especially, the poor. Here, the IMF and World Bank play a major role. To ensure that the banks will not again get into trouble, they have made new loans dependent on what they've called 'structural adjustment'. Structural adjustment aims to ensure that poor countries can keep servicing their debts and take on new loans. This is achieved by promoting exports, which yield the foreign exchange needed for debt servicing, and reducing government expenditure. In the latter, special emphasis is put on cutting 'non-productive' or 'social' spending on such items as health care, education, and social security. Other favorite targets are investment in social infrastructure, such as sanitation, drinking water supply and low cost housing. Also, subsidies are lowered, especially on basics like food and medicine.

Slashing health and education budgets and subsidies on food and medicine hits hardest at the poor. Whereas wealthier people can turn to private schools, doctors and clinics, the poor have no such option. Also hard hit is the lower middle class, especially civil servants. In many countries, their real wages today are only a fraction of what they were twenty years ago. In some countries, mass lay-offs have taken place; most of those loosing their jobs have little hope of finding new, reasonably paid employment.

To give an impression of the scale of these effects, take the example of the African country of Ivory Coast. World Bank research on the consequences of structural adjustment showed that from 1985 to 1988, the first three years of the program, demand for goods and services declined by 30%. At the same time, the number of poor increased from 30% (2.8 million) to 46% (4.8 million) of the population.

Thus, the cost of the debt problem, and of the measures taken to prevent it from endangering the rich nations' banks, is carried by the poor and the lower and middle income groups. Among the poorest, this has contributed to widespread malnutrition, an increase in child mortality, and reduced access to education and health care services. Also, drinking water supply and sanitation systems have deteriorated. Those affected most severely are children:

the United Nations Children Fund, UNICEF, estimated in 1992 that each year approximately half a million children die as a result of decaying health services, water supply and sanitation.

In short, structural adjustment is good for banks and other creditors. But it is fatal for development, especially in the longer run. It wrecks the chance of tens, if not hundreds of millions of people to live healthier, more productive lives. Moreover, by depressing local demand, it reduces the opportunities for business and thus, for balanced economic growth. And it does not even begin to solve the debt problem, as is shown by the fact that the developing countries' debt load is still rising.

Bad government

The above may create the impression that Third World poverty is primarily due to the international financial institutions, private banks and rich nation's governments. There is, however, an even more primary cause: bad government in the poor countries. Partly, this is due to a lack of managerial skills. Yet that's only a partial explanation for the misspending of loans, wasting of resources and poor financial management that so typifies many Third World governments. Another major factor is the indifference towards and deliberate mismanagement of public resources by the ruling political and economic cliques. Indeed, the question should be asked to which extent bad government is due to ineptitude, and to which extent it is purposeful. The answer depends on what is understood by good and bad government. If the performance of rulers is measured by the well-being of the population they govern, most do a poor job. If, however, performance is measured in the benefits rulers obtain for themselves, their families and their close associates, they are doing great.

The ruling cliques of most poor countries have been singularly successful in increasing their own wealth at the cost of their fellow citizens. Favored means are graft, kickbacks, abuse of monopolies, and many other forms of corruption—including the downright plundering of national treasuries. Some of the gathered wealth is consumed or invested locally; much is transferred to Swiss bank accounts or other safe havens in the rich nations. A former Nigerian leader has estimated that African leaders have stashed away some $20 billion in foreign, especially Swiss, bank accounts.[16] Similarly, in December 1994 a government commission in Brazil estimated that within a one year period, civil servants, contractors and suppliers had illegally grabbed about 40% of the total budget for improving the country's economic infrastructure—some $20 billion in all. A large part of this money also ended up in foreign bank accounts.[17]

In all, the damage done by local leaders and their associates with plundering their countries' treasuries and national resources runs into the hundreds of billions of dollars. The money involved would be enough to pay off most of the national debts of the countries involved. As the case of Brazil shows, theft and corruption have become a way of life not only for dictatorial leaders, but for large parts of the upper layer of Third World societies.

Another problem is spending priorities. Most notably, over the last decades the leadership of the poor nations has wasted huge amounts of money on the military. For the 1981-1989 period, for example, the developing countries spent some $620 billion on arms and other military expenditure.[18] Even half that amount would have gone a long way in providing the poor in the nations involved with education, clean drinking water, basic health care, and sanitation. It doesn't happen: in 1990, the developing countries spent 70% more on arms than on education and health care combined.[19]

Lack of responsibility also shows in the attitudes of the upper layers of society towards paying taxes. In the rich nations, with top income tax rates varying between 30 and 60%, the wealthy contribute significantly to their countries' treasuries. In the poor countries they do not. Property and income taxes are usually low, and more often than not evaded. Take the Philippines. In this island nation, where 70% of the population lives below the poverty line and servicing the foreign debt takes up 40% of the national budget, the rich face an income tax of no more than 3%. Even that minute proportion is seldom paid.

In other poor nations taxes may be higher, but actual payment won't differ much from the Philippines. As a rule, tax collection services are hopelessly understaffed and underpaid. More effective tax collection would be perfectly possible with only minor investments in training and equipment—which would earn themselves back in no time. However, the politicians and bureaucrats who should originate and carry out such measures stand to lose the most by doing so. Therefore, fighting tax evasion is, to put it mildly, not a priority.

Aid

So what about aid? Since 1960, the developing world has received about $1.4 trillion in so-called development assistance; by 1995, the annual amount stood at about $60 billion.[20] Unfortunately, as we've seen, the way most of this money has been spent has not helped in eliminating poverty. Ill conceived mega-projects such as roads, bridges, harbors, power plants and irrigation projects did little to improve the situation of the poor. They were, however, highly profitable for the companies carrying them out—which as a rule, were based in the country financing the project. Thus, most of the money spent flowed straight back to the donor nation.

More than from these 'productive investment' projects, the poor would benefit from programs aimed at satisfying basic human needs: primary education and health care (including family planning), safe drinking water, sanitation, and small loans to help them set up some kind of productive activity. Overall, however, only some 10% of development assistance goes to such programs.[21] World Bank figures show that in 1988, of all aid to low-income countries, a mere 2% went on primary health care, and only 1% on population programs.[22] One reason of this is that such programs offer few opportunities for business from rich countries. Another may be that for the political and economic leadership of the receiving countries, the chances for graft and kickbacks are smaller.

'Development assistance' that certainly won't help the poor is military aid. Still, some countries include it in their official aid figures. Thus, a quarter of the official development assistance given by the U.S. consists of military supplies. The reason why such aid is given is, of course, political rather than moral. Political considerations are also obvious in the choice of countries that receive the most aid. For example, about a third of U.S. aid goes to Israel— hardly a developing country.

With all this, the amount of aid given by the rich countries is shamefully low. Although an annual amount of $60 billion may seem like a lot, it is only about one third of a percentage point of the rich countries' gross national product (GNP). Only the small Scandinavian countries of Denmark, Sweden and Norway come close to, or give more than 1%. Germany provides only 0.36%, for Britain and Japan the figure is about 0.30%. The U.S. gives only 0.18% of its GNP in foreign aid—and even that is being cut back.

The responsibility of the rich nations

'So what's all this to us?' readers from rich countries may say. 'Why should we pour more of our tax money into helping the poor if those most to blame for poverty are their own leaders? You can't hold us responsible for Third World misery!'

Not directly, perhaps. But indirectly, yes. The rich countries *are* for an important part responsible for much of the misery in the poor countries. Misdirected aid—much of it given in the form of loans—and faulty loan policies can be blamed as much on lenders as on borrowers. The structural adjustment policies used to manage the debt problem are imposed by the international financial institutions, which are controlled by the rich countries' governments. Therefore, the citizens of those countries are at least partly responsible for the fact that hundreds of millions of people, especially women and children, are robbed of the chance to improve their lives.

Yet the responsibility goes further than that. The rich nations have played a key role in bringing to power the poor nations' incompetent and abusive rulers. This support dates back to the 1950s and 60s, when the Cold War was at its height. It may have been 'cold' for North Americans and Europeans, but was unbearably hot for millions of people in poor countries. Over the last few decades, dozens of civil wars were fought that were spawned and fanned by superpower rivalry: Nicaragua, El Salvador, and Guatemala in Central America, Angola, Mozambique, Ethiopia and Somalia in Africa, and Vietnam, Cambodia and Laos in Asia. Many more countries were affected by so-called 'low intensity conflicts' between governments and small guerilla movements. All these conflicts brought social and political upheaval, repression, and economic decline. Invariably, those who suffered most in these conflicts were the poor.

Within the framework of the Cold War, then, the rich countries have done a great job in providing inept, corrupt leaders with the means to grab and stay in power. They were supported even though it was known that they abused and stole public resources, including grants and loans from the rich countries, and suppressed any attempt at legitimate opposition. As long as they served the political, military and economic interests of the rich nations, they could count on military, economic and political support. As the rich countries' governments who gave this support were democratically chosen, its citizens carry at least some responsibility for the consequences.

Shared interests

The above could well serve as the basis for a moral appeal to aid the poor in improving their fate. Yet that's not the main purpose of this chapter. Rather, it is to illustrate that the middle and lower income groups in the rich countries, and the poor and the middle class in the poor countries, are hit by the same global forces. That means that they have the same interests in countering those forces, and in pressuring the decision makers that promote them to change things around.

At first sight, workers in rich and poor nations may appear to have opposing interests. Most notably, there is the competition for jobs that are increasingly transferred from rich to poor countries. Yet from a long term perspective, their interests overlap. Poverty in poor countries means low demand for goods and services. That reduces business opportunities and therefore, job creation—in rich as well as poor countries. Moreover, the focus on exports, resulting from the poor countries' need to pay their debts, makes for growing competition in international markets. Among others, this leads to 'social dumping': the selling of products at rock bottom prices, made possible by excessively low wages and by the failure to comply with even the most basic of workers' rights.

Social dumping is fostered by free trade. Thus, workers in both rich and poor countries suffer the consequences from the policies advocated by mainstream economists and in their wake, by politicians and media pundits. In the rat race of international competition, workers at all levels will have to work harder for lower wages, and face increased risk of loosing their jobs.

In the rich countries, labor unions developed when workers understood that they shared the same overall interests—even though they were competing for jobs and were working for competing companies. Those interests were reasonable wages and benefits, and adequate working conditions. They also saw that the only way to further those interests was through cooperation. Similarly, workers of rich and poor countries should come to see that, rather then compete for the favors of investors and employers, they must cooperate. Only thus can they obtain their fair share of the gains of economic and technological development.

Chapter III

THE ENVIRONMENT

Most people will say that if one thing is more important than their economic situation, it's their health. Most experts will state that our health is linked closely to what happens in our environment. It is odd, then, that for most people, the environment is only a matter of secondary importance. Apparently, the link between our health and our environment is insufficiently recognized.

Take the U.S.: few people are so preoccupied with their health as Americans. Yet the environment was ranked only 13th on a list of fourteen issues people indicated as important for the 1992 presidential elections.[1] Economist and Newsweek columnist Robert Samuelson is a typical representative of the view of many opinion makers as well as large parts of the public on environmental issues. It is therefore worthwhile to take as a starting point in establishing the environment's importance a 1992 *Newsweek* column in which he condemns 'environmentalism's rhetorical excess' as 'wild exaggeration or simple dishonesty'.[2] Comparing the numbers of dead from environmental problems with those from World War II and Cambodia's civil war, Samuelson concludes that: 'On any scale of tragedy, environmental distress is a featherweight'. The question is, is Samuelson correct, or are there indeed valid reasons for the concern of environmentalists and scientists?

There are three related types of what Samuelson calls 'environmental distress'. First, at world level, the most basic natural resources, air, water and soil, are increasingly contaminated. Moreover, large areas of agricultural soil are degrading so rapidly that the capacity to feed the world is threatened. Second, natural ecosystems, especially rainforests and wetlands, are rapidly disappearing. Not only are these areas home to many plant and animal species, they are also climate regulators and sources of clean air and water. Third, many raw materials upon which modern society depends, notably oil and various metals, are being consumed so quickly that within a few generations there will be nothing left.

Mr. Samuelson's remark that 'environmental distress is a featherweight on the scale of human tragedy' seems thin, considering that in the cited column he does not explicitly give an estimate of the number of people affected by environmental problems. Yet consider this citation: 'A recent report from the World Bank estimates that more than one billion people lack healthy water supplies and sanitary facilities. One of the results is the death of three million children annually, two million of which the World Bank judges avoidable.' Obviously, Mr. Samuelson does not count these deaths as due to 'environmental distress'. Yet he should. Water is not inherently unhealthy: it becomes so because of contamination. Water is polluted by chemical and, especially in the developing countries, organic wastes. The three million deaths this causes each year among children would hardly qualify as 'a featherweight on the scale of human misery'.

Yet the toll of 'environmental distress' is much larger. The disruption of natural ecosystems such as forests and wetlands, for example, causes the disruption of water cycles and natural drainage systems. Each year, the resulting floods take hundreds, if not thousands, of lives. Moreover, the disappearance of forests contributes to prolonged droughts. Both flooding and drought cause the losses of crops and livestock, which can lead to famines. Even if people do not die from hunger, lack of food makes them more susceptible to disease. Again, it is especially the children who suffer: their physical and mental development is impaired, and child mortality rises.

Another serious problem is soil degradation. It threatens the livelihood of hundreds of millions of people who depend on small scale farming. Lower yields make for less food and lower incomes. As mentioned, that results in a higher susceptibility to disease and thus, higher death rates, particularly among infants. When agricultural production falls to levels where the family can no longer feed itself, people move to urban areas in search of a better life. There, they face new health risks, posed by the often appalling sanitary conditions in city slums.

A third form of 'environmental distress' that takes a heavy toll is exposure to chemicals. The World Health Organization (WHO), the Food and Agricultural Organization (FAO) and the International Labor Organization (ILO) estimate that, worldwide, each year tens of thousands die of direct contact with agricultural and industrial chemicals. Some disasters make the press, such as the 1984 accident in a Union Carbide plant in Bhopal, India. It resulted in an estimated 5,000 deaths; many more people were impaired for life. Yet accidents like Bhopal form only the top of the iceberg. To give an impression of the extent of the problem, consider this: in 1994 the Chinese Xinhua news agency reported that in 1993 alone, 500,000 Chinese workers had been exposed to toxic substances leaking from industrial installations.[3]

The above figures apply to the incidental exposure to chemicals, usually through accidents. Much more widespread, however, are the deaths and impairments resulting from the long term, continuous exposure to dangerous substances. The Russian academy of medical sciences has estimated that half the Russian drinking water supply and a tenth of the food supply is to some extent contaminated by chemicals. As a result, 11% of newborn children suffer birth defects, and 55% of school age youths have exposure-related health problems.[4]

A lesser known form of pollution is the burning of wood. In the developing world, hundreds of millions of people depend on it for cooking. The World Bank estimates that 300 to 700 million women and children are affected by the indoor air pollution caused by woodfires. Especially in towns and cities, industrial fumes also take their toll. All in all, worldwide, 1.3 billion people are exposed to dangerous quantities of particles and smoke.[5] Again, the consequences are illness and, in many cases, premature death.

It is difficult to make an estimate of the total number of victims of 'environmental distress'. It would perhaps be possible to calculate the number of 'direct' deaths: those occurring shortly after exposure. But it is almost impossible to count the non-fatal and fatal illnesses (including cancer), the premature deaths, the stillbirths and the miscarriages that appear months, years or even decades after exposure has taken place. Still, the above given estimates point to the likelihood that each year, millions of people die as a direct or indirect consequence of environmental degradation, whereas hundreds of millions see their health affected.

The overwhelming majority of the direct victims of environmental degradation live in the poor countries. Thus, at first sight Mr. Samuelson's 'featherweight' contention would appear to gain in strength when applied to the rich nations. That, however, he does not, by making the comparison with World War II and the civil war in Cambodia. He may be right when he states that in the rich countries the number of 'direct' deaths from environmental causes is relatively small. Still, we don't really know how many deaths from diseases such as cancer are caused, partly or entirely, by environmental factors. What is certain, however, is that today, in the rich countries, the number of casualties from war or economic causes is even smaller.

Air

In the rich countries, as said, the main health hazard is the exposure to chemicals that are emitted into the air, water and soil. The principal problem is that we know little of the effects these substances have on the human body. Of the some 65,000 chemical compounds used commercially in the rich nations, information on toxicity is available for only 1%. Moreover, each day three to five new chemicals enter the market. Over 80% of these new substances have not been tested for toxicity.[6]

In general, it is known that environmental pollutants have the potential to undermine vital bodily functions. Especially vulnerable are the nervous system, the endocrine system (which regulates hormones) and the immune system. For example, one third of the 197 substances to which a million or more American workers are exposed have the potential to damage the central nervous system and the brain.[7] Yet exposure limits are the exception rather than the rule. Of the 50,000 industrial chemicals currently in use, occupational standards have been set for less than 700. Every day, European industries discharge more than 2,000 different chemical compounds into the Rhine river—a source of drinking water for 20 million people. The EC directive on drinking water, however, covers just 66 pollutants.[8]

Testing for toxicity is also a problem. More than 700 chemicals have been detected in U.S. drinking water, 129 of which are considered dangerous by the Environmental Protection Agency. Nonetheless, drinking water is regularly tested for only 14 of these contaminants.

On the positive side, the rich countries have been successful in reducing the most blatant forms of pollution, such as soot, sulphur dioxide and lead (from leaded gasoline) in the air, and organic wastes in rivers and lakes. As a result, in most of the U.S., Canada, Northern Europe and Japan, the air and surface water are considerably cleaner than twenty years ago. Yet even these successes are relative. Gains in reducing the level of pollution per volume— for example, per gallon of sewage—are offset by the increase in the quantity of emissions. For example, over the last 20 years, in the U.S., contamination per volume unit of water has been reduced by half, at a cost of some $100 billion. Yet in the same period, the amount of sewage has doubled. Therefore the net effect of this enormous investment has been zero.[9]

In any case, much more drastic reductions are called for. In 1992, European health organizations estimated that in spite of progress already made, emissions of such contaminants as nitrogen oxides and ammonia would have to be reduced by another 60 to 80%. For other major pollutants, figures ranging from 70 to 90% applied. Yet the opposite is taking place: of most substances the released quantities are still rising.

When adding rapid population growth and expanding consumption in the poor nations, the picture becomes even more worrisome. With current growth rates, the world population will double over the next 60 years. In this same period, average consumption per person will rise two-and-a-half times. That amounts to a five-fold increase in total consumption. This means that, just to keep environmental damage at today's levels, emission per unit of product would have to be reduced by 80%.[10]

Keeping emissions at today's level is not enough, however. The damage now caused by pollution is already too high. In the U.S. alone, air pollution costs as much as $40 billion annually in health care and lost productivity. In agriculture, crop losses due to air pollution have been estimated at between 5 and 10%—implying annual losses of $3.5 to $7 billion.[11] The cost of air pollution in Europe (including Russia West of the Ural) has been estimated at some $30 billion a year.[12]

The developing countries produce much less contaminating emissions than the rich countries. Yet because pollution control is almost non-existent, those emissions are often more harmful. Consequently, in the cities where most factories and power plants are established, contamination is worse than in the rich nations. The rapid increase of traffic and the use of poor quality engines augment the problem further. As a result, the most polluted cities in the world are now found in the poor countries: Mexico City, Santiago de Chile, Cairo, Bangkok, Shanghai and Sao Paulo. As these cities continue to grow, pollution levels are bound to increase further.

There are two forms of air pollution that do not yet form major health problems, but may have enormous implications in the future. One is the depletion of the ozone layer in the earth's atmosphere. It is caused mainly by the emission of substances called chlorofluorocarbons (CFCs). An important function of the ozone layer is to serve as a filter for ultraviolet (UV) radiation from the sun. One of the consequences of the depletion of the ozone layer is, therefore, increased exposure to UV rays. Scientists have found that this increases the risk of skin cancer, can cause cataracts and blindness, and can weaken the immune system. UV radiation can also damage crops, livestock and wildlife. According to participants in a 1992 conference on ozone depletion, in Copenhagen, Denmark, the latter may well be the greatest danger. Plants must spend energy in rebuilding cells destroyed by UV radiation, at the cost of crop growth and yields. The growth of algae and plankton, the small organisms in the seas and oceans on which all other sea life depends, could also be affected. This could lead to greatly reduced fish catches.

● The second long term environmental threat is global warming. It could occur as a result of the burning of oil, coal and gas to generate energy for industry, transport and heating. Burning releases gasses in our atmosphere, especially carbon dioxide (CO_2). These gasses interfere with the reflection of solar heat from the earth's surface back into space. Thus, the heat is trapped inside the atmosphere—as in a greenhouse. As a result of this, many experts fear that in the coming decades world temperatures might rise several degrees. That could cause the melting of huge quantities of polar ice, which would raise sea levels. Land that is now at or just above sea level would inundate. Rising temperatures could also lead to climate changes that could turn areas formerly apt for agriculture into deserts. Moreover, they could cause an increase in the number and strength of storms, hurricanes and cyclones.

Water and soil

One good thing about air: there's enough to go around. That cannot be said for fresh water. For many people, water scarcity is an even bigger threat than pollution. Over 200 million people, living in 26 countries, face water shortages. In parts of Canada, the U.S., China and India, current shortfalls will increase strongly in the near future. In Kansas, for example, lack of water is estimated to put 75% of existing crop land out of production by the year 2025. In parts of California, water shortages have led to limits being set on the growth of urban areas. In India, by the turn of the century water requirements are projected to exceed dependable supplies in every single state. Yet enormous amounts of water continue to be wasted: up to half the fresh water humanity uses is lost due to shoddy irrigation practices.[13] According to the United Nations Environmental Program, by the year 2050, some 50 to 60% of the global population will face water shortages.[14]

As happens with water, soils are affected by both pollution and losses through inadequate use. Soil pollution is caused by the same factors as the contamination of water and air: the dumping of hazardous waste. Until recently, these materials were disposed of in garbage dumps, on industrial terrains, and on just about any other location producers saw fit. In the rich countries, the health hazards of these dumps became a public concern only in the late 1970s. Regulations were drawn up that obliged business to dispose of their toxic waste in ways that would not endanger public health.

Yet great damage has already been done. In the U.S., up to 1990, some 50,000 hazardous waste landfills had been detected. Some 20,000 of these have been listed as a threat to human health. Two-thousand of these sites require immediate clean-up at a cost that, according to the Environmental Protection Agency, could top $100 billion. In former Western Germany some 6,000 dump sites have been labelled dangerous. Eight hundred of these are deemed a threat to public water supplies. The cost of merely cleaning the latter has been estimated at $10 billion.[15]

The above mentioned costs only refer to the most urgent cases. For decontaminating all the hazardous waste sites encountered in North America and Northern Europe up to 1992, the total bill could run to well over $1 trillion. For the U.S. alone, a figure of $750 billion is cited; new terrains are added to the list almost daily.[16] Moreover, in many countries companies continue with the inadequate disposal of industrial waste, as laws and regulations are not adequately enforced.

In Eastern Europe and in the poor countries, toxic waste dumping has hardly begun to be considered for the problem it is. The situation there is comparable to that in North America and Northern Europe in the 1960s. Dangerous waste products are dumped haphazardly, without restrictions, even in residential and natural areas. For Poland, for example, there are estimates that put the annual amount of toxic waste dumped into unregulated sites at 20 million tons. The lack of control has also attracted polluters from the rich countries. Instead of appropriately processing and disposing of their wastes at home, they find it cheaper to ship it to poor countries, where it can be dumped without questions asked.

Although soil pollution can be a major threat to human health, the areas involved and the number of people directly at risk are relatively small. The greater danger of soil pollution lies in the possibility that toxic substances are washed out of the contaminated soil and pollute ground and surface water. Thus they can spread far outside the original dump site, contaminating the water supply of thousands or even millions of people. In former Czechoslovakia, for example, some 90% of the wells that yield water for home and industrial consumption have been polluted to some extent.

Worldwide, the loss of agricultural soil poses an even greater danger than pollution. Inadequate use of agricultural land and the cutting of forests cause erosion and other forms of soil depletion. Each minute, close to 20 acres of the world's agricultural land are lost. In 1991, 17% of the total vegetated area on earth was found to be degraded to a larger or smaller extent.[17] Twelve million km^2—a surface larger than that of the u.s. and Mexico combined—has been affected so severely that rehabilitation is beyond the capacity of the individual farmer.[18]

The degradation problem is greatest in the developing countries. In India, for example, 800,000 km^2 is affected by erosion; six billion tons of top soil are lost annually.[19] Ethiopia loses one billion tons of top soil each year. If current trends continue, over the next 25 years in this country alone, an area the size of former East Germany will change into desert.[20] Yet erosion is also a problem in the rich countries. In England and Wales, 37% of the agricultural land is subject to erosion; some 4 billion tons of fertile top soil are lost each year. Similarly, due to inadequate management, the wheat belt in Canada has lost half its organic material and continues to erode. In Australia, 23% of range and cropland is affected.[21] According to the u.s. Department of Agriculture, in the u.s. one third of the total area used for crop production, some 430,000 km^2, suffers from unacceptable levels of erosion.[22]

In dry regions, erosion is followed by the formation of deserts. The United Nations Environment Program holds that 30% of the world's land surface is threatened by desertification. Three-quarters of this area, some 33 million square kilometers, is already moderately affected. If present trends continue, the total area of arable land will be halved within a century. Already, the cost of land degradation in dryland regions, in the form of reduced crop yields and livestock productivity, is huge: worldwide annual losses are estimated to run to more than $42 billion. Losses in the more humid regions, including the u.s. corn belt and Europe's most productive regions, have yet to be estimated.[23]

Land is also lost to faulty irrigation practices. Excessive use of water, due to high losses before the water actually reaches the crop, causes salinization and water logging. The United Nations World Commission on Environment and Development has estimated that as a result, each year some 10 million hectares of irrigated land are abandoned.[24] Salinization greatly reduces agricultural potential, as many crops do not tolerate soils with a high salt content. The areas affected are large: for Argentina, for example, the Commission indicates that nearly 50% of the irrigated area has salinization problems. For Iran and Iraq, a figure of 40% is given; in the u.s., 25-30% of the total irrigated area is either threatened or already affected by salinization.[25]

Garbage

Another growing environmental problem is the disposal of the ordinary waste products of modern society. In rich as well as poor countries, the amount of refuse produced by business and households keeps growing every year. Getting rid of it becomes increasingly difficult. The capacity of landfills is limited and in many, more densely populated areas, will soon run out. Also, using landfills is dangerous, as harmful wastes mixed with ordinary garbage may seep into ground water that is used to produce drinking water. One u.s. survey found that of 50 sites studied, 40 had contaminated ground water. Also, landfills are susceptible to the build-up of explosive gases, particularly methane. In England and Wales, according to a 1989 estimate, 1390 landfill sites posed a risk of explosion—756 of them within 250 meters of housing.[26]

Another problem with landfills is that they take up space. In densely populated areas, this is in increasingly short supply. Transport to farther off areas is expensive, and people there are unlikely to welcome the refuse produced by others. This augments chances that wastes are dumped in sparsely or uninhabited, ecologically sensitive areas. Thus, natural habitats on land and in rivers, lakes and coastal areas can be destroyed.

The production of garbage is directly related to the level of wealth. In the rich countries, cheap energy and raw materials, high labor costs and love of ease have created a throw-away society. For many products, replacement has become easier and cheaper than repair, and disposal after use is simpler than returning or cleaning. For suppliers, of course, replacement is attractive as it implies higher sales. Yet the toll in terms of tons of garbage produced and the consumption of (finite) raw materials, including energy, is high. Moreover, new products imply the need for more packaging, another major contributor to the garbage mount.

The poor countries produce much less refuse than the rich ones. To be sure, the upper layers of society throw away as much as their counterparts in the rich countries. But the poor produce only very limited amounts of garbage. The average Nepalese, for example, generates only one-fourthiest as much refuse as the average u.s. citizen. In addition, the poor reuse and re-cycle a significant portion of the refuse originated by the upper layers of society—often in remarkably creative and inventive ways.

Cultural differences also play their part: in a nation like the Netherlands, with a standard of living not much below that of the u.s., the per capita production of waste is only half that of the u.s. That shows that without major effort or sacrifice, it is possible to reduce the quantity of garbage significantly. Apparently, the 'American way of life', determined for an important part by the seemingly endless supply of space, energy and raw materials, is more prone to waste production than the somewhat more sober lifestyle of the Dutch.

Minerals

The minerals most widely used in modern society, such as oil, gas, coal and metals, are finite, non-renewable resources. At our current rate of consumption, the bottom of the treasure trove is coming in sight. In 1989, known supplies for oil would, with consumption remaining constant, last another 40 years, those of gas 60. Fortunately, new supplies are still being discovered: at present, most experts agree that non-discovered reserves will prove to be roughly equal to the supplies now known.[27] That means that even when consumption is maintained at current levels (which is unlikely) oil supplies would run out in about 80 years, those of gas, in 120. Coal supplies are more abundant: based on current usage, supplies should last another 230 years.

Except for iron, aluminum and, possibly, titanium, metals are also scarce. The known reserves of copper, zinc, lead and tin have been estimated to run out in as little as 20 to 40 years. Again, new supplies are likely to be discovered, but consumption is also increasing.

Scarcity will stimulate the search for alternatives. Moreover, as prices rise, consumption will be reduced. Thus, supply and demand will be balanced. But steep increases in prices will have serious economic consequences. The poor may not be able to afford either the scarce materials or their alternatives. Reduced industrial and agricultural output could lead to economic crises and large scale food scarcity. Chances of this coming true are greatly enhanced by population growth. By the time the shortages will occur, the world's population is likely to have nearly doubled, from the current 5.7 to approximately 10 billion.

Ecosystems

The world has a wide variety of ecosystems, such as tropical rain forests, mountain and dry land forests, wetlands, savannas, prairies, deserts, and coral reefs. Over the centuries, and in particular during the last hundred years, people have invaded and disrupted all but the most remote of them. As a result, almost all remaining natural areas are today seriously threatened. Of the six billion hectares of forest on the earth's surface, only 1.5 billion is still untouched. Europe has practically no original forests left; in the U.S., without Alaska, only 15% remains. Since the turn of the century, the developing countries have lost half their original forests. In countries like the Philippines and India, less than 5% remains. Worldwide, an average of 17 million hectares of tropical rain forest, about 1% of the total remaining area, is lost each year. If this rate continues, all tropical rain forests will have disappeared by 2040.[28]

The world's wetlands—marshlands, swamps and bogs—form another seriously endangered ecosystem. About half the world's salt water marshes have already been destroyed by drainage and development schemes.[29] In the U.S., more than half the salt and sweet water wetlands have been sacrificed to development. Countries rich in wetlands such as Malaysia and Finland have done likewise. The Philippines sacrificed, between 1920 and 1988, more than 80% of its huge areas of coastal mangrove forests.[30]

There are, of course, moral arguments for preserving the last natural areas. Practical considerations, however, should also carry weight. Wetlands, for example, act as a buffer against floods, tidal waves and storms, absorbing flood waters before they reach higher ground. Some 65% of the fish caught for human consumption is spawned in wetlands, and they play a vital role in cleansing water of pollutants and sediment. Wetlands also house many species of plants and animals. Rice is a wetland plant, as are the oil palm and the sago palm. The remaining wetlands contain many wild varieties of these crops. Some day, their unique traits could serve to create resistance against pests and diseases that affect varieties cultivated by farmers.

Forests are perhaps the most valuable natural ecosystem. By converting CO_2 into water and oxygen, they help counter global warming. They also contain an enormous variety of plant and animal life, only a few percent of which has been investigated in any detail. Yet even this minor proportion has already given us a wide variety of food crops, medicines and other useful products. Thus, tropical rain forests provide the raw materials for 40% of modern medicines as well as thousands of traditional cures. Citrus fruit, banana, cassava (a root crop that is the staple for hundreds of millions of people in the tropics), quinine, cocoa, rubber, chickens and pigs all originated in tropical forests. Some products, such as various kinds of nuts, ingredients for medicines, and wicker, are still harvested from the forest. If the small proportion of the forest's life forms that have been studied have already yielded so much, there are sure to be useful species among the tens of thousands that have not yet been investigated.

Another important role of forests is that through the production of moisture, they regulate local and regional climates. The large scale felling of trees makes humid climates drier and hotter. Forests also serve as sponges, absorbing heavy rainfall and releasing it gradually in streams and rivers. When the trees are no longer there to store the water in the soil, streams and rivers are reduced to a trickle in the dry season, while turning into raging torrents during the wet. The run-off fouls up rivers and settles in natural and artificial reservoirs, reducing irrigation and energy generating capacity. Sediment is also deposited in river beds and deltas, where it can block the free flow of water, thus increasing the risk of floods. In South Asia, for example, the increased incidence of flooding has been linked to the deforestation that has taken place on the slopes of the Himalayas.

Agriculture

Traditional forms of agriculture resemble natural ecosystems in that they're highly varied. Worldwide, local farmers have, over the ages, domesticated hundreds of crops and selected thousands of crop varieties, all uniquely adapted to their environment. Modern industrial agriculture, however, has greatly reduced the number of both crops and varieties. Enormous areas are sown with only one or two high yielding strains which, to realize their productive potential, need large amounts of chemical fertilizers and pesticides.

The unnatural character of industrial agricultural production has negative environmental consequences. The prolonged use of chemical fertilizers, pesticides and heavy machinery affects soil composition. The affected land has a lesser capacity for water absorption and is more susceptible to erosion. The use of chemicals eliminates the natural enemies of insects that attack crops; without such predators, crops become even more dependent on pesticides. Moreover, insects, bacteria and viruses develop resistance to agro-chemicals, requiring a continuous search for new, stronger formulas.

Perhaps the most alarming consequence of industrial agriculture is that diversity is replaced by uniformity. True, in the 1960s and 70s the replacement of hundreds of traditional crop varieties with a handful of modern,

higher yielding ones led to spectacular increases in production—a phenomenon that has come to be known as the 'Green Revolution'. Yet the adoption
of these new varieties, and subsequent disappearance of thousands of traditional strains, entails great risks. Scientists continuously try to outsmart the
insects, bacteria and viruses that attack crops by creating new, resistant varieties. But not only do pests adapt quickly to new chemicals, they also manage
to overcome resistance in new crop strains. The question is how long scientists can stay ahead in this race. One major problem in this respect is the very
disappearance of traditional crop varieties. This has resulted in the decima-
tion of the genetic base from which breeding traits can be drawn. This
weakening of the genetic base, combined with the growing dependence on
just a small number of crops and crop varieties, and with the amazing capacity of crop pests to adapt, threatens global food security. If a major pest in
rice, corn, wheat or another major crop would overcome the resistance of the
most widely used strains, and would itself develop resistance to the available
pesticides, massive crop failures could occur. This, in turn, could lead to
large scale starvation and famine.[31]

It is doubtful, then, that the impressive gains in productivity obtained in
industrial agriculture can be sustained. Certainly, industrial agriculture is
not sustainable from an environmental point of view. Moreover, because of
the problems of pest resistance and the loss of genetic material, society's almost total dependence on industrial agriculture puts humanity at great risk.

The failure to address the problems

The above is only a very brief sketch of the problems of environmental degradation. It shows, however, how the way we treat the environment can affect
our health and our future. So why is pollution, the squandering of finite raw
materials, and the destruction of natural ecosystems allowed to continue?
The answer is that to do something about it is not economically attractive.
The conversion to more sustainable forms of agriculture would eat into the
profits of transnational companies producing agro-chemicals and seeds of
modern crop varieties. Measures to protect the environment and use finite
resources more prudently cost money and could slow production. That
means lower profits and economic growth. Politicians, interested primarily in
the next election, don't make short term sacrifices for long term gains. Mainstream economists are even less willing to forego economic growth for such

airy notions as the well-being of future generations. This attitude is strengthened when, as happens with the Greenhouse effect, there are still doubts as
to the extent of the damage that can be expected. The standard view is that as
long as it has not been decisively proven that major damage will occur, no
costly action should be taken.

This attitude is comparable to that of a person who is in a high risk category for heart trouble, yet smokes, drinks and eats to his heart's delight 'because it is not 100% certain I will actually get a heart attack'. Anyone would
call such behavior totally irresponsible. Yet at the political and economic
level, that is exactly the attitude regarding the environment. What's worse is
that the above person is only deciding about his own life. Our leaders, on the
other hand, are taking, or failing to take, decisions that are likely to affect all
people, of present as well as future generations.

What we're dealing with here is a conflict between short term private interests and the long term common good. Business wants profits, politicians
want votes. If those have to come at the cost of the environment, so be it. Environmental regulation is called for only when consumers or voters would be
affected directly by its absence. The art, however, is to keep the costs as low
as possible. In practice, that means that pollution, waste and the destruction
of ecosystems can continue as long as they do not generate a public outcry.
Investment in environmental protection is feasible only when the political
and economic costs of not doing so would be higher, for example, through
voter rejection or consumer boycotts.

Yet the problem is not only one of unwilling politicians, business people
and economists. It is also that of a public which is not yet disposed to make
sacrifices for the environment and thereby, for the long term common good.
There is, so it seems, a kind of stand-off between the public and its leaders.
Politicians, fearing rejection by voters and business, don't mention environmental problems, and the public prefers not to hold them accountable for
their lack of vision and character. The few politicians who propose to make
the needed sacrifices are solidly trounced at the polls. Thus leaders can rightfully say that measures to counter the problems are not 'politically viable'.
The environment loses out—and so do future generations.

Some people may argue that the above is too negative a view. They will
point out that since the 1960s, public concern about pollution and disappearing ecosystems has increased enormously. They will note that business
has reacted to those concerns, and cite examples of companies that have
significantly improved their environmental records. They may even men-

tion cases of companies performing better than required under government regulations.

All this is valid—to a certain extent. Yet environmental concern, among the public as well as politicians, has had its peak. Now, partly as a result of economic insecurity and stagnating incomes, attention for the environment is diminishing. As for business, in spite of environmental sweet talk results are still measured in profits rather than in contributions to a cleaner environment. Only in as far as the latter increases profits can real progress be expected. Sometimes, environmental measures allow companies to present a 'green image' to the public. That may be good for sales and profits. Most pollution control measures, however, are expensive and eat into profitability. Whenever that is the case, the latter will be the main priority.

In the developing countries, the prospects for a reversal of environmental degradation are even worse than in the rich nations. One reason is that the resources needed to address the problems are much scarcer. A second problem is, as in the rich nations, the attitude of the political and economic decision makers. Many are prone to present environmental protection as a typical rich man's issue. Only the rich, so politicians, business people and economists argue, can afford to ponder the long term consequences of the loss of natural ecosystems. Poor countries, however, have no choice but to exploit the little they have. People need land, business needs profits. Governments need the tax income and hard currency obtained by exploiting natural resources—if only to serve the debts to the rich nations. Only if a much higher level of economic development has been attained, so it is argued, can the poor countries afford to tackle environmental issues.

The skepticism of Third World political and business leaders towards environmentalism is to a certain extent understandable. For decades, the rich countries have recklessly polluted the global environment and squandered the world's resources. By doing so, they have achieved a level of economic development that is unparalleled in history. Now, those same countries tell the developing nations to forego economic growth in order to protect their natural resources. In the meantime, to please lumber companies and real estate developers, they continue to destroy the few remaining original forests and wetlands at home. Now *that's* hypocrisy.

However, by taking the moral high ground the leaders of the poor nations miss the main point. That point is *not* that the rich countries have no right to tell poor countries what to do with their natural resources. It is that the poor nations themselves will pay the highest price by far for the destruction of their environment. They will suffer, much more than the rich countries, the consequences of local and regional climate change: drought, erosion, desertification, shortages of irrigation water and hydroelectric power, and flooding. Also, poor countries are likely to pay a higher price than the rich nations for global warming. Most experts predict that the severity of storms, droughts and floods is likely to increase more in the tropics than in temperate climates. Estimates hold that due to climate changes, food production in the poor countries could decline by some 10%. On the other hand, in the temperate zones where the rich countries are located, global warming might actually boost yields.[32]

Even if this were recognized, there remains a still greater barrier to be overcome. It is similar to that already mentioned for the rich countries: the short term interests of the ruling economic and political cliques. Local business leaders and politicians benefit from the razing of natural ecosystems, and from the possibility to produce goods and services without being hampered by environmental regulations. The same goes for transnational companies. Moreover, globalization drives governments to impose as few limitations as possible on companies that have to compete in world markets. It is likely, therefore, that if current economic trends continue and the reckless pursuit of even greater wealth by the ruling economic and political cliques is not countered, the environment will continue to lose out.

Chapter IV

CRIME

Every day, millions of people become victims of crime. Almost everyone has either experienced it personally, or knows someone in his or her immediate surroundings who has. Many victims suffer the consequences for the rest of their lives. People are worried: U.S. citizens consider crime the most serious issue facing the country.[1]

Overall, crime appears to be on the rise. Between 1970 and 1993, the number of murders in the U.S. rose by more than 50%, from 16,000 to 24,500 per year. Whereas overall violent crime rates (murder, attempted murder, assault and armed robbery) were stable in the first half of the 1980s, the second half of the decade showed a 22% increase. During the 1980s, West Germany experienced a relatively modest rise in violent crime of about 10%. But for countries like The Netherlands and England, increases of over 80 and 90%, respectively, are reported.[2]

It is often assumed that most criminals come from the lower income groups, and that most of their victims are rich. That, however, is not usually the case. In the U.S. a disproportionate share of murders is committed by and against young black males; their rate of victimization is ten times as high as that of young white men.[3] Both victims and offenders originate in the poverty ridden neighborhoods of the big cities. The rich, living in better protected surroundings, are much less likely to become a victim of violent crime than the poor.

In many poor countries, the rich take crime for granted. People have gotten used to protecting themselves from the outside world with private guards, high walls, bars and security systems. The poor have no such protection. Usually, criminals can operate unhindered, as the poor suffer more harassment than protection from law enforcement agencies. Often, their only protection is that there is little to get from them. Yet poverty makes any loss, however small, more difficult to handle.

Types of crime

For most people, what comes to mind when discussing crime is the type that affects people personally, such as theft, robbery, assault, rape and murder. I'll call this form of crime *direct*, to show that it involves a direct relation between offender and victim. A special form of direct crime is what I'll call *official* crime: violence enacted by representatives of the state. Official crime coincides with what are usually called 'human rights violations'. The fact that imprisonment, physical and psychological abuse, torture and murder are practiced by the state does not mean they are legal. All human rights violations are against international law and almost always, they are also against the laws of the nations where they are committed. Yet without a well-functioning and independent judicial system, those who are responsible for official crime can act with impunity.

As opposed to direct crime, *indirect* crime does not involve a direct relation between offender and victim. Instead it victimizes the state and as such, society as a whole. Examples are offenses such as tax evasion, money laundering or the abuse of public funds. Indirect crime may be committed by individuals, but also by organizations. When committed by legal organizations it is called *corporate*, when perpetrated by illegal organizations, *organized* crime.

Because indirect crime does not affect people directly, most of the public does not view it as a major issue. Perhaps they would if they realized the cost of this form of crime to society. Especially tax evasion and corruption have, over the last few decades, taken on gigantic proportions. Several studies have estimated that, annually, as much as $300 billion is whitewashed—that is, brought from the illegal into the legal financial circuit.[4] Total criminal turnover for 1996 has been put at approximately $1 trillion dollar, half of it generated in the u.s.[5] Most of this money comes from the drug trade and indirect crime. Of course, not all illegally obtained money is whitewashed: many funds are re-invested in other illegal ventures, spent on goods and services paid for in cash, or hoarded outside the financial circuit. Therefore, the total amount of illegally obtained money is likely to be much higher than the above sum.

For the poor countries, the most damaging form of indirect crime is corruption. During the fifth International Conference on Corruption, held in 1992 in Amsterdam, Italian sociologist Pino Arlacchi stated that the largest sums of illegally obtained money are not in the bank accounts of drug traders or arms dealers, but in those of the heads of state and other high government officials of developing countries. This group has captured a big portion of the hundreds of billions of dollars provided in aid and loans by the rich nations: Arlacchi gives an estimate of about $200 billion over the 1976-1985 period. But corruption is not limited to the rich and powerful: it has also pervaded the lower levels of society. The amounts involved are lower, but the number of offenders is huge: whereas dictators, politicians, high bureaucrats, and police and army brass rake in millions, lower ranked officials scrape together amounts varying from tens to hundreds or thousands of dollars. Overall, annual losses due to corruption are likely to run into the hundreds of billions of dollars.

Many rich countries also have widespread corruption. In Europe, the further South one goes, the more pervasive corruption becomes—with, as has been shown recently, Italy as a prime example. In the Northern countries, corruption is checked better than in the South. There appears to be a more developed system of checks and balances, and a stronger watch dog function of the press. Most important, there is more public rejection of both large and small scale corruption. Still, indirect crimes like tax evasion are widespread even in Northern Europe. The Germans, with their reputation for orderliness and obedience to authority, have been estimated to evade taxes to the extent of some $30 billion a year.

The main victims of indirect crime are, as is the case with direct crime, the lower income groups and the poor. In Chapter II, we've already seen how especially in the poor countries, the lack of government income that results from corruption and non-payment of taxes leads to a shortage of funds for public education and health care. This affects both the health and the economic opportunities of the lower income groups. Thus, both the existence and continuance of poverty can be linked at least partially to the indirect crime perpetrated by the upper layers of society.

In the rich countries the consequences of indirect crime are less severe. Still, the funds involved would go a long way in addressing urgent problems such as deteriorating public education and health care systems, urban poverty, direct crime, pollution and a decaying infrastructure. Therefore, in the rich countries also the problems encountered by the less well-off and especially, the growing army of poor people, can be linked at least partly to indirect crime.

Some forms of indirect crime make direct victims. For example, the breaking of pollution control laws can cause health problems for people exposed to the toxic materials involved. Also, worldwide thousands of people are hurt every day because laws relating to labor safety are not adhered to. Similarly, the breaking of laws on child labor, minimum wages and working hours affects the well-being of millions of people—and again, particularly the poor.

Causes of crime

The question of why people engage in crime is a complex one. That is because crime takes on so many forms, and because the circumstances in which it occurs are so diverse. Moreover, the motives people have for committing crime vary enormously. Sometimes, they may not even be clear to the offenders themselves. Recent research has found that at least some impulsive criminal behavior has biological causes, and therefore appears to be more a medical than a social or psychological problem.

In addition to biological factors, there are two main factors that make a person opt for staying within the law or going outside it. One is moral qualms: some people won't perpetrate a crime because they think it's wrong. The second is the fear of a response from society: punishment.

Ideally, a person would not commit a crime because of moral objections: it is felt to be wrong to benefit oneself at the cost of others, be they individuals or society at large. Society has laid down certain rules, and to break those rules implies doing damage to the social order. Thus, one complies with the law because one is convinced that it is the right thing to do, as it is a precondition for society to function.

This is far from a generalized attitude. Many people consider that they get a raw deal from society. Therefore, they feel few misgivings about breaking its rules. Poor citizens may think that the law exists mainly to protect the interests of the rich and powerful: whereas they get away with murder, the poor always seem to end up getting the short end of the stick. Such feelings of alienation are bound to grow when the inequality in society increases. It becomes even worse when the poor see their chances for improvement diminish, while the rich flaunt their increasing wealth. The more people perceive they have little chance of escape, the greater the hostile feelings towards society. The greater the frustration, the greater the risk that these feelings lead to direct crime.

Many people have a less hostile attitude towards society. However, they do not see laws as part of a regulatory system that allows people to live together more or less harmoniously. In principle, they abide only by laws that they feel should be complied with, because not doing so would directly harm other persons. But they have few misgivings about breaking laws that they see as pointless or unfair, or as contrary to their interests. Also, they may figure that law-breaking that does not directly hurt others is not morally wrong. Therefore, they will have few inhibitions about committing indirect crime—especially if it's done on a small scale and if they feel they can get away with it. A good example of this kind of attitude is cheating on income tax returns.

Another state of mind that can lead to crime is a feeling of being above the law. The law is seen as something to maintain order under normal people, but can be bent to help superior individuals reach their goals or protect their interests. This attitude is typical of wealthy and powerful offenders, including those responsible for official crime. It easily takes on extreme proportions: the people or groups involved show few reservations in having their opponents jailed, tortured and murdered. Especially in many poor countries, the wealthy have come to consider the use of violence against people they perceive as a threat to their interests as something normal.

Lack of moral qualms, then, makes people *potential* law breakers. So what brings them to actually engage in crime? Two factors stand out: motive and risk. The most obvious motive to break the law is, of course, the desire for profit. In the case of official and organized crime, this desire often combines with the urge to preserve wealth, power and privilege. Another, less frequent motive for crime is hate and the desire for revenge, in response to real or imagined wrongs. Much of the violent crime that results from alienation falls into this latter category. Alienation can also create a 'culture' of crime, in which committing violence is a precondition for being accepted by a group one identifies with. Instead of personal profit, the prime motive for crime then becomes what the people involved consider social advancement.

After motive, the most crucial factor in determining if people break the law or not is risk: the chance of getting caught, and the consequences if that happens. Risk is a particularly crucial factor for 'calculating' potential offenders: those that balance the potential benefits against the likely costs. If there is a major chance of getting caught, and if punishment is so severe that it outweighs the potential benefits, a calculating offender will not commit the crime. On the other hand, if chances of getting caught are slim, if punishment is lenient, and if the benefits to be obtained are worthwhile, such offenders may engage in crime when an adequate opportunity presents itself.

This is the case especially for what is usually called 'white collar' crime: non-violent crime for monetary profit, engaged in by relatively wealthy and well-educated people.[6]

By those that do not consciously balance benefits and costs, the severity of punishment and the chance of being apprehended are not considered. That is the case, for example, for those who commit crime in an emotional state, or who lack the capacity to clearly analyze in advance the possible consequences of their behavior. To a lesser extent, it applies to people who are pressured by their peers into breaking the law. And finally, it goes for those who perceive their situation as so bleak that they feel they have little to lose even if they are caught. If conditions trigger the right emotion, and if the right occasion presents itself, such people are likely to engage in crime—whatever the punishment or the chances of getting caught.

Solicited and unsolicited crime

Up to now, we have talked about direct crime, which makes unwilling victims, and indirect crime, which makes unknowing ones. There are also acts that, although forbidden by law, are carried out with the full consent and on the request of the supposed victims. I'll call this 'solicited crime': crime committed to satisfy the illicit demand of certain individuals or groups. Examples are the trade in and use of drugs, prostitution, and illegal gambling. To varying extents, one could also include in this category abortion, euthanasia, various forms of sexual behavior, and even suicide—where such practices are illegal.

Obviously, solicited crime is even harder to fight than unsolicited crime, as both supplier and consumer will want to hide their actions from the authorities. Thus, the production and consumption of the goods and services involved is pushed underground. The ensuing absence of regulation and the huge opportunities for profit make solicited crime an attractive option for criminal individuals and organizations. That's why the mainstay of organized crime is solicited crime: drugs, prostitution, gambling. In an unregulated market, a free-for-all ensues in which every means is used to enhance business—including direct crime.

Rising crime rates make it clear that the 'fight against crime', announced on numerous occasions by many different governments, is largely unsuccessful. That's not surprising. The way most governments wage the 'war against crime' is by expanding police forces and building more prisons. In the U.S., Canada, Britain and France, spending on the police, the trial system and prisons takes up 80% of law enforcement budgets. Only 1% is spent on preventive measures, such as the counseling of children and youths growing up in high risk environments, or the rehabilitation of convicted offenders.[7]

In theory, expanding the police force could increase the risk for offenders to get caught. That could help prevent crime. Usually, however, proposed increases in law enforcement budgets are not nearly large enough to reach that goal. Besides, law enforcement systems are notoriously inefficient: for the rich countries, it has been estimated that only some 5% of all crimes are actually tried in a court of law.[8] Only a fraction of these trials results in convictions. It can safely be assumed that in the poor countries these percentages are even lower. Therefore, increasing police forces and prison capacity by, say, 10 to 20%, is unlikely to change crime rates significantly.

The fight against crime also fails because even when offenders are convicted, their punishment is often no incentive to change for the better. Prison is supposed to make violators reconsider their actions, and bring about a change in attitude that will keep them from breaking the law in the future. The term 'correctional center' reflects this idea. In practice, however, imprisonment has little or no correctional effect. In the rich nations, between 40 and 60% of those sentenced return to crime within a three year period.[9] The 'law of the jungle' atmosphere that predominates in many prisons, and the resulting physical and mental abuse by fellow prisoners and sometimes, prison staff, leads only to a further estrangement from society. In such an environment, those who were not hardened criminals when they went in are likely to come out as such. Worst of all, even when a prisoner comes out intending to go straight, the stigma attached to a stay in prison makes it difficult or impossible to find employment. Therefore, for many ex-convicts there appears to be little choice but to return to crime.

As said, fear of punishment can keep people from breaking the law. This is the deterrent function of such penalties as fines, imprisonment and capital punishment. People consider the negative consequences of breaking the law and decide that it isn't worth the risk. This deterrent effect, however, only applies to calculated crime: offenses committed after the possible benefits have been compared with the risk of getting caught and punished.

The alienated, low status offenders who are responsible for most direct crime only rarely calculate the effects of their actions. Therefore, for them the deterrent effect of severe punishment is limited or none. Much indirect crime, however, is calculated. That includes corporate and organized crime. In those circles, therefore, high risk and severe punishment will be effective deterrents. Yet particularly for indirect crime chances of getting caught are small—so small, that they do not deter calculating offenders. Also, in many countries most forms of indirect crime carry such lenient sentences that even when offenders are caught and sentenced, the benefits of committing the crime are greater than the costs. Obviously, in such a situation the deterrent effect of punishment is lost altogether.

So what are the prospects? Direct crime is likely to continue to increase as the gap between rich and poor widens, and the lack of opportunities for disadvantaged groups continues to augment. Increasingly, the norms and values that regulate social life will lose their meaning for those who see their situation worsen and their hopes frustrated, while the upper layers of society flaunt growing wealth. On the other hand, among the rich the growing gap will further reduce their already weak attachment to the concepts of social equity and equal rights. Even more than before, they will rationalize the unequal distribution of wealth and opportunities, arguing that they deserve what they have because they are mentally and morally superior.

Indirect crime is likely to increase due to technological development and the opening up of national borders. Computer crime, tax and business fraud, and the entry of organized crime in legal economic activities are growth sectors in a world in which finance and business are increasingly internationalized. In the meantime, understaffed law enforcement agencies continue to operate primarily at the national level. As chances of getting caught are reduced, indirect crime becomes more attractive—a strong incentive for calculating offenders.

Most worrisome is that in today's world, there is so little incentive to fight indirect crime. Those hardest hit by it are largely unaware of the consequences, and powerless to do much about it. Those who benefit are often members of the same economic and political decision makers that control government and thus, legislation and law enforcement. That is, the people who should take the initiative for measures to fight indirect crime belong to, or are closely linked to, the very groups that benefit from it. It is therefore hardly surprising that measures for full international cooperation in tracking and recuperating illegal funds, and in establishing who owns what where, are not even discussed—let alone proposed and implemented. The banking secret continues to exist in countries such as Switzerland and Luxembourg, as do tax havens like Liechtenstein, Panama, the British Channel Islands, the

Dutch Antilles and the Cayman Islands. International action aimed at abolishing such havens for illegal funds would help enormously in fighting indirect and solicited crime. So would international agreements giving governments a complete overview of their citizens' assets abroad. But since those who would have to set up such cooperation have too great an interest in maintaining the *status quo*, they are highly unlikely to take action.

Chapter v

GOVERNMENT

Political systems

Government consists of two components: the political system and the civil service. In the former, policy is made. In a democracy, this is done by elected officials. The civil service, or the government bureaucracy, carries out those policies. This is done by appointed officials.

Political systems can be separated into totalitarian and democratic ones. The key distinction between the two is accountability. In democratic states, leaders must allow freedom of expression and organization, subject themselves to elections, abide by the law, and submit to an independent judicial power if they do not. Totalitarian regimes are much less accountable. They do not hold elections, or they arrange them so that their victory is ensured. That happens through vote rigging, falsifying election results, or not allowing opponents to put themselves forth as candidates. Also, totalitarian regimes suppress freedom of expression, and ban organizations they consider as opposed to their interests. Moreover, they control the judicial branch, which is turned from a check on to an instrument of power.

The legitimacy of a totalitarian government, then, rests not on a mandate from the people, but on control of the means of power. If totalitarian leaders don't give up power voluntarily, the only way to have them do so is through violence. That is difficult, since a key attribute of a totalitarian regime is that it controls the military and police forces. Nevertheless, over the last decades many totalitarian regimes, especially in Latin America and the former East Bloc, have made way for governments chosen in more or less free elections. With the partial exception of East Asia, the democratic system has become the international norm.

To be truly democratic, that is, a true expression of the people's will, the periodic elections on which a democracy is based must be free and fair. 'Free' implies that in principle, any person should have the right to vote as well as the right to run as a candidate—individually or as a member of a political party. Of course, certain limitations of a practical nature will have to be applied, such as a minimum age for voters and candidates. Such limitations, however, should never be linked to political convictions. 'Free' also refers to every voter having the possibility to vote without restraint, that is, without pressure to vote for one or another person or party. For that, it is essential that elections be secret, so that determining who voted for what or whom becomes impossible.

The 'fair' in 'free and fair' refers, on the one hand, to the absence of fraud in the casting and counting of votes. On the other, it refers to all candidates or parties receiving equal opportunity to make their viewpoints known to the public. For that, they should have equal access to the media.

In many supposedly democratic nations, this is not the case. In some, the media are at least partly controlled by the party in power. Consequently, opposing viewpoints are not given attention or are distorted in an attempt to influence voters. Candidates of the opposition are slandered while information unfavorable to the ruling party and its leadership is suppressed. Often, public funds are spent to promote the ruling party and its politicians.

In other nations, with the U.S. as the most obvious example, elections are unduly influenced by money. Money determines the possibilities for political parties and candidates to present their viewpoints to the public. The more money, the better the chance to influence voters. Obviously, this system favors the interests of wealthier interest groups, who can financially support the political party that best suits them. Thus, in the U.S., considered by many, and especially its own citizens, as the shining example of democracy, the democratic process has degenerated. The key element of fairness in elections, that is, the right of voters to an even-handed information supply, has been sacrificed to the power of money.

Democratic political systems are preferable over totalitarian ones—for both moral and practical reasons. Let's start from the premise that all human beings have equal rights. In that case, a system in which people are free to decide for themselves who should lead them, and in which those given power can be held accountable, is morally superior to systems where this is not so. Totalitarianism can therefore be justified only in systems in which some people are deemed or deem themselves superior to others.

From a practical viewpoint, the advantage of democratic systems is that periodic elections provide the opportunity to sack poorly performing leaders. That makes for an effective check on those given power. The knowledge that the next election is never far away will make officials listen to their voters, and will give them a strong incentive to gain and maintain their support.

Too great an influence of voters on policy making, however, can be harmful for effective governing. Electorates usually consist of a wide variety of individuals and groups, each with their own specific interests. Some of these interests may coincide, others may be contrary. The task of a government is to develop and carry out those policies which best serve the majority, while minimizing any negative effects for the rest of the population. In other words, governments have to strive for the common good. Unfortunately, because of the many conflicting interests in modern society, striving for the common good will almost always involve harming the interests of some people. Moreover, people's short term interests may be contrary to their long term ones—making governing even more complex.

A good example is the need for pollution control. Especially in the longer run, environmental protection will benefit public health and well-being. Moreover, it is essential to ensure a decent quality of life for future generations. Pollution control, therefore, serves the long term common good. However, in the short run the measures involved will raise the cost of consumer products. This is contrary to the short term interests of most people. Up to a point, people are willing to pay somewhat higher prices—for their own long term well-being and for the long term common good. However, the increased production costs resulting from pollution control can also cause some companies to go bankrupt. The resulting job and financial losses will seriously hurt those involved. Because for them the sacrifice is so much greater, they are likely to oppose pollution control and thereby act contrary to the long term common good.

The tension between short term interests and the common good is especially strong when a politician is tied to a small constituency. In systems that choose a representative per electoral district, state or province, elected officials are bound to put the interests of their constituency before the national interest. Often, the two do not coincide. Take the example of a military installation that, from the point of view of national security, is superfluous. The national interest would dictate that it be closed. In the district where the facility is located, however, it is important for the economy, providing employment and a market for locally produced goods and services. Representatives of the district will therefore oppose closure—taking at heart their constituents' concerns rather than the national interest.

In theory, in such a situation the representatives from other districts, forming the majority, would see to it that the national interest is served. After all, they would have no direct interest in keeping the facility open. In practice, things work differently. Political deals are made in which representatives of different districts support each other on decisions of interest to their specific constituencies—even if they're detrimental to society at large. For example, in exchange for support from representative B to keep the military installation in representative A's district open, representative A supports B in opposing stricter environmental standards that would affect industries in B's district.

The limitations imposed by constituencies are even stronger in international politics. With a lot of goodwill, the U.N. could be considered as the institution charged with looking after the global common good. But there is no international electorate, and therefore no pressure on politicians to watch over the interest of all of humanity. In the international arena, therefore, the national interest takes absolute precedence. Consequently, the U.N. is used as a forum for promoting national rather than global interests. Effective international measures can be taken only in the rare cases where the national interests of all major powers and of a majority of other nations coincide. In other cases, the U.N. can at best help solve conflicts between member nations. It lacks, however, the power of national governments to initiate and implement policy.

That is a worrying situation in a world where global problems require global solutions. Protecting the environment, the rational use of natural resources, eliminating poverty, fighting crime, and arms control can only be dealt with effectively at the international level. Far-reaching international agreements, adhered to by all major nations, are needed. Yet with all these issues short term national interests, such as the cost of the measures needed to address the problem, conflict with long term global ones. Since it is the national electorate that brings in votes, not humanity as a whole, short term national interests prevail.

The hierarchy of interests

Politics, then, is determined by the existence of a hierarchy of interests. At the top of the hierarchy are the interests of the politicians themselves. Next are the interests of their party, followed by those of the special interest groups that support the party and its candidates. Fourth come the interests of the constituency the politicians represent, fifth, the national interest. In sixth place we find regional interests: for example, those of the rich nations, Europe, or the Islamic countries. In seventh, there are the interests of all of humanity, whereas level eight represents the interests of future generations.

Figure 1 depicts the hierarchy of interests on a vertical scale of priorities. Parallel to this scale, one of time spans is presented. The further down one goes in the hierarchy, the longer the time span over which interests are measured: from a few years at the level of the interests of politicians and political parties, to a few decades for future generations.

The hierarchy of interests depicted in Figure 1 makes it clear why small groups of people can succeed in blocking measures that are of interest to humanity as whole. For example, it explains why a special interest group of (large) farmers and agro-industries in the rich countries succeeds in forcing politicians to maintain a very expensive system of agricultural subsidies. Its very cost makes it run counter to the national interest. Also, by subsidizing ecologically damaging forms of production, the interests of future generations are hurt. Yet these drawbacks at levels five and eight are less important than the interests of farmers at level three.

FIGURE 1 *The hierarchy of interests determining political decision making*

Highest Priority		*Short Term*
1	Personal interests of politicians	
2	Interests of political party	
3	Interests of special interest groups	
4	Interests of constituency	
5	National interests	
6	Regional interests	
7	Interests of humanity —present generations	
8	Interests of humanity —future generations	
Lowest Priority		*Long Term*

Similarly, the hierarchy of interests helps explain why the international community, and notably the rich countries, do so little to counter gross abuses of power by leaders of poor nations. The beneficiaries of such action would be people from other nationalities. In the hierarchy, their interests are almost at the bottom. The costs (financial and, in case violent intervention would be needed, wounded and dead) would have to be borne by the nations undertaking such action—at the fifth place in the hierarchy. An erroneous assessment of the cost could result in voter disapproval. That would harm the interests of the responsible politicians, and of the political party they represent. Here, we're at the top of the hierarchy. With interests at this level threatened, those at the bottom cannot but lose out.

Conflictive engagement

Of course, most politicians will deny that there are conflicts of interest with their electorate and society at large. After all, they like to be considered as the selfless defenders of both the interests of their constituency and the national common good. To promote this image, they tend to emphasize conflicts of interest lower in the hierarchy—notably, between their own and other nations. The question is, however, if people from different countries really have conflicting interests.

There are good reasons to assume that's not the case. Throughout history, people have shared a common interest: to be left in peace. They had nothing to gain and much to lose in wars which were started by leaders looking to increase their status, power and wealth. They suffered terribly from the murder, rape, and pillage engaged in by soldiers. Moreover, they had to endure the taxes imposed upon them to finance their lord's wars, the forced conscription into their armies, and the general social and economic upheaval that accompanied war.

Today's civilians also have nothing to gain and a lot to lose from conflict. They don't profit from the endless bickering between politicians either. As in the past, people benefit from peace and order and a rapid, fair and practical solution of the problems society faces. At a time when many global issues have to be addressed urgently, they would profit from effective international cooperation, aimed at furthering the common good. Instead, what they get is a continuous struggle to defend national short term interests.

The problem here is that political conflict is in the interest of politicians. To understand why, look at the past. The rulers of old, of course, did not care much about the common good. Policy was made not for the benefit of people but for emperors, kings and aristocrats. Its goal was to further the power of a ruler while weakening his opponents. The interests of the citizenry were hardly taken into account.

Today, in the modern, democratic nation state, things are supposed to be different. Now, so we're told, our leaders and representatives formulate and carry out policies in the interest of the people. Yet in practice, the goal of politics has remained the same: to satisfy the needs of those who govern. Traditional rulers have simply been replaced by politicians. As the aristocracies of old, they are perfectly willing to further their own purposes at the cost of the interests of those they govern. The main difference is that they're less frank about it.

To lend credibility to the claim that they serve the public interest, politicians deny that people worldwide share common interests. Instead, they justify their position, power and privilege by presenting the world as a place of conflict. By nature, so they say, people are at each others' throats: to compete for scarce resources, or to fight out some innate, beastly aggression. They argue that in a world of strife, professional and capable politicians are essential for protecting people's interests. They present politics as a contest in which, for the benefit of their electorate, they are forced to engage. By giving themselves the status of expert players they create a market for their skills. By making problems as complex as possible, they keep themselves in business and raise the value of their expertise. Thus politics becomes 'conflictive engagement': a permanent battlefield in which each party, applying all available means, will try to get maximum benefits at minimal cost.

The conflictive engagement that marks today's politics, then, does a great job in providing politicians with what they want: power and status. However, it runs counter to the aim of government, which is to further the common good. Considering the problems society faces, politics is a profession practiced according to outdated principles. Conflictive engagement was and is functional only to serve the personal interests of rulers. Today, however, it has become an obstacle to effective action for global development.

Of course politicians will say, with some justification, that even today, there are still many leaders who resemble the rulers of old. They will argue that the only way to keep such regimes in check is through conflictive engagement. Still, that does not explain why conflictive engagement also dominates the relations between democratic countries. Nor does it account for the continuous bickering that marks politics within most democratic nations.

Politicians will also explain conflictive engagement as a result of differing opinions on how to tackle society's problems—at the national as well as the international level. Although again, there is some validity to this argument, it has lost most of its relevance with the collapse of socialism. Today, disparity between programs of most mainstream political parties and candidates is small. Certainly, they don't justify the way in which in many countries, candidates go at each other's throats in election campaigns. Thus, the fading of the struggle between the world's two major ideologies has exposed politics for what it really is: a vehicle to further the interests of its practitioners.

So are all politicians intent only on promoting their own well-being, at the cost of the general public? Not necessarily. The problem is that even those of good will are forced to play the game once they are caught up in the system. The only way to survive in the political arena is to play along—and play as dirty as one's opponents. Politics will be changed only by changing the goals and the rules of the game. To foster the cooperation needed to address today's problems, the change needed is so fundamental that the word politics might no longer apply.

The lack of vision

Fostering the long term common good, that is, ensuring the well-being of future generations, calls for investment in the future. Environmental protection and the fight against poverty will pay for itself in the longer run, but require sacrifices now. Politicians should convince voters of the need to make those sacrifices or, more positively put, investments. For that, they need credibility and vision. Among today's politicians, both are sorely lacking.

The lack of credibility is due to many factors. The constant bickering between politicians that results from conflictive engagement is one. Poor governing, leading to misuse of public funds and growing national debts, is another. Backroom deal-making, pork-barrel politics and politicians abusing their privileges is a third. And, in many though not all countries, outright corruption has reduced politicians' images to nil. The resulting loss of credibility puts politicians in an awkward position to ask voters to invest for the common good. They simply lack the moral standing and the trust of the public which is needed to ask for any sacrifice at all.

Among the public, there is a widespread feeling that people receive too little in return for their tax money. Lower and middle income groups experience lower living standards, rising crime rates, and a declining quality and higher cost of public services. The wealthy also feel they are shortchanged.

The dwindling quality of public education and health care makes them turn increasingly to private suppliers of such services. As a result, they are less and less inclined to foot the bills of government. Thus, both groups come to perceive government as an entity serving politicians and bureaucrats rather than the public. The state is no longer seen as the institution that looks after the common good, but as an entity meddling in people's lives.

Besides credibility, politicians and governments lack another even more basic element: a vision on where society should head. This is not only a problem of politicians: the same is valid for scientists, opinion leaders, and other authorities who should provide society with intellectual leadership. It appears that anything resembling a vision of the kind of society we want has vanished. Lacking such a vision, politicians have turned economic growth into the fetish of modern politics.

Of course, there are practical reasons for striving for economic growth. In the past, as we've seen in Chapter 1, it meant more jobs and wealth for most people. Moreover, growth is needed to pay off national debts—a major concern of rich as well as poor countries. Also, economists and politicians argue that economic growth is needed to pay for measures to protect the environment and fight poverty. Yet questions such as who benefits from growth, whether it makes the environment and people healthier or just the opposite, and whether well-being is increased because of it—if not for all, then at least for a majority—are hardly asked. Growth has become an end in itself, rather than a means to achieve more well-being for society as a whole. It has become such a fixation that policies are feasible or not only to the extent that they increase or decrease the gross national product.

The emphasis on growth has given economists and economic science a major role in policy making. Unfortunately, though, mainstream economic science fails to take account of the long term common good. For example, it does not consider the cost to society of having to replace oil as a source of energy. Neither does it take account of the long term cost of pollution, such as higher costs for purifying drinking water, cleaning up toxic waste dumps, higher health care costs and reduced crop yields. Nor does it consider the long term economic cost of lost productive potential, as a result of cutbacks in education and health care budgets.

As a result of these shortcomings, main-stream economists tend to dismiss the social, environmental and long term economic consequences of short term economic policies. That's bad enough from a scientific viewpoint. But it becomes disastrous when, without recognizing their shortcomings, economists recommend policies with consequences that go way beyond the realm of economics. The final blame, however, lies not with the economists, but with the politicians. After all, it is their lack of vision that has put economists on the pedestal from which they announce their single-minded gospel. And much more so than economists, politicians have the responsibility to employ a more ample vision on the common good than economic growth.

Bureaucracies

Politicians make policy, government bureaucrats carry them out. In addition, they take care of many routine matters: the outcome of policy made in the past. All these actions together are what is called public service; those who carry them out are public servants.

In practice, many public servants, especially in the poor countries, have forgotten what their name stands for. Instead, their prime and often only interest is their own. They can ensure their jobs by creating more tasks for themselves, and increase their power by elaborating ever more detailed rules. Such excessive regulation can hinder economic, social and political development. It can also be a source of corruption.

There are many forms of official corruption. One is personal enrichment through stealing state funds. Another is selling services that should be provided free. A third form, closely related to the second, is favoring some persons over others—because they're family of friends, or because they pay for the privilege.

Corruption harms society in several ways. We've already seen how stealing from public coffers leaves less money for important services such as public education, health care, and fighting crime. The sale of services and favoritism hurt the interests of all those not favored. Sometimes, they can lead to people obtaining permission for actions that are illegal and contrary to the public interest. For example, environmental regulations can be waived, resulting in pollution and the razing of natural areas. A major drawback of favoritism in appointments is that it increases the chance that state institutions come to be staffed with incompetent officials, even on key positions.

In many countries, particularly poor ones, the public accepts favoritism as a fact of life. The concept of impartiality, that is, the right of each citizen to equal treatment, is typical of the liberal democratic principles that Europe and North America developed over the last two centuries. To many non-western cultures, however, this principle is alien. Especially in Africa, the creation of nations and of the bureaucracies to govern them has not changed traditional ties: those with family, village, clan, region or tribe. Ties at these levels are much stronger than those with other citizens, with whom the only thing in common is that they happen to be citizens of the same nation.

This hierarchy of ties, or allegiances, runs counter to the right of equal treatment for all. Traditional allegiances call for the favoring of next of kin, fellow-villagers, clansmen and tribesmen over others. Tradition makes favoritism not only socially acceptable, but also socially expected behavior. It is accepted even by those who are disadvantaged by it: they would do the same if they had the opportunity.

There are also other reasons for corruption. In many poor countries salaries of civil servants are so low that they're practically forced to ask for and take bribes. Payment for services that should be given for free or not at all (for example, giving a permit where it is not warranted) has become a simple matter of survival. For that reason also, the public accepts corruption as a fact of life.

Another reason for corruption is that there are so many bureaucratic rules, regulations and procedures that the use of shortcuts is essential. Helping citizens to cut through this bureaucratic tangle becomes a valuable service. The need of civil servants (for additional income) then combines with that of citizens (for help in cutting through red tape) to create a climate in which corruption can flourish.

Thus described, corruption perhaps does not look so bad: both civil servants and those making use of their services benefit. However, one should remember that, as indicated above, favoring some implies handicapping others. Those who will benefit are those who can pay: the wealthier and therefore, more powerful citizens. The poor, without the means to pay for the services they are entitled to, suffer. Especially in cases of conflict between rich and poor, where a neutral official should do justice, corruption will resolve the conflict in favor of the wealthy. Thus, throughout the world the poor lose disputes over access to land or water—even though from a legal perspective, they are in their right. Corruption in state bureaucracies, including the judiciary, then, contributes to poverty while benefitting the well-to-do.

Part 2

SOLUTIONS

'*A federation of all humanity, together with a sufficient means of social justice to ensure health, education, and a rough equality of opportunity, would mean such a release and increase of human energy as to open a new phase in human history.*'

H.G. Wells, historian

Chapter VI

SUSTAINABLE ECONOMIC GROWTH

A global investment program

In Chapter I, I mentioned the growing gap between productivity and demand as one of the key economic problems facing society today. Growing
competition forces companies to cut jobs and cap wages. This dampens demand, which leads to even fiercer competition. That, and technological development, causes productivity to rise, meaning that even fewer workers are
needed to satisfy demand. More people lose their jobs, wages are lowered,
and demand is stifled further. Thus the downward spiral will continue.

To reduce the gap between productivity and demand, demand should be
stimulated. Economists usually recommend to do so by increasing people's
after-tax income, through tax cuts. Not such a bad idea, if the beneficiaries of
such cuts are the lower income groups. Unfortunately, as we've seen, the tax
cuts most economists and politicians propose favor the rich much more than
the poor. After what happened in the 1980s that should, from any reasonable
point of view, be out of the question: it would be patently unfair to shovel
even more wealth to the rich. Besides, it wouldn't do the trick: consumer demand would not rise very much, as this group is fairly small in numbers and
consumption levels are already high. Instead, the extra income from tax
breaks would further the speculative investment discussed in Chapter I. That
would mean an even bigger extraction of capital from the productive sectors
of the economy than is the case today.

Tax cuts that would mostly benefit lower income groups would be a better
idea. The amount of income over which no income tax is due could be increased. Also, the percentage to be paid over the lowest income tax bracket
could be reduced. The problem, however, is that because all taxpayers would
benefit from such measures, even minor changes would be very costly. Take
the U.S.: if we put the number of income earners at 150 million, tax cuts that
would provide all of them with $500 in extra expendable income would cost

$75 billion. That would either lead to new budget deficits, or force even greater cuts in public spending. In the latter case, at least part of the cuts would likely be made in those areas that are important for sustainable development: education, public health, fighting crime and poverty, environmental protection, and economic and social infrastructure. That would not only be contrary to sustainable development, but also lead to a reduced demand for goods and services from the state—offsetting at least partly the gains in consumer demand.

The above problems could be overcome if the cost of the tax cuts could be covered through higher taxes on the wealthy. From the point of view of fairness this would be an attractive option: the rich would be returning, to the rest of society, some of the enormous wealth that has been sluiced to them since the 1980s. Still, tax cuts for the lower and middle income groups would not effectively address our prime economic problem: the growing gap between productivity and demand. True, consumer demand would rise, but a $500 increase in expendable income would not have the major impact on demand that is needed. On the one hand, that's because the sums involved are small compared to the overall size of the economy. On the other, it is doubtful that this extra income would indeed be spent on the purchase of goods and services. Especially the middle income groups, faced with growing economic security and rising costs for (higher) education, health care and retirement plans, are more and more prone to save rather than consume. Besides, the middle and lower income groups still have debts to settle. Obviously, if the proceeds from tax cuts are used to increase savings or to pay off debts, the effect on demand will be minimal.

Finally, one should ask if increasing consumer demand is the most adequate way for ecologically sustainable growth. The answer is no. In the rich countries, more consumption of the present kind would make our society even less sustainable than it is today. Finite materials would be used up faster, emissions of pollutants and Greenhouse gasses would increase, as would our garbage disposal problems.

My proposal for fostering demand, therefore, would not be to do so by stimulating more consumption of consumer goods and services. Instead, demand should be stimulated through a global investment program for sustainable development. In line with the objectives of sustainable development, this program should aim to make good quality education and health care accessible to all, to make the global economy ecologically sustainable, and to improve the world's social and economic infrastructure in ways that allow all people to enjoy an acceptable standard of living.

This global investment program should consist of five components. The first would aim at the conversion of today's economy into one in which our natural resources are used in a sustainable manner. It would involve global measures for pollution control, the recycling of wastes, and the conversion from non-renewable to renewable energy, such as wind, sun and hydro power. Also, it would focus on building a worldwide infrastructure for water management, to resolve current and future shortages of water, control flooding, and make more water available for irrigation. The latter would be of major importance for increasing food production and raising farm incomes, especially in poor countries. A further point of attention would be the protection and reclamation of soils through reforestation, terracing, drainage and other measures. All these themes will be looked at in some more detail in Chapter VIII.

The second component of public investment would aim to ensure to the extent possible that all people lead healthy and productive lives. For the young, this implies to prepare them as well as possible for their entry into social and economic life. For adults who, in some way or another, have been pushed to the margins or out of society, it would mean to help them reintegrate. The main areas of attention would be day care for the very young, education, health care, law enforcement, the rehabilitation of offenders, and care for the elderly. Special attention for babies and toddlers and better health care and education are, as we'll see in Chapter VII, of key importance for people's social and economic development. Also, in Chapter IX, we'll see how these measures would contribute to lowering crime rates—as would better law enforcement and, especially, rehabilitation.

The third public investment component would be to improve the world's economic and social infrastructure. With economic infrastructure, the emphasis would be on improving transport and communications in both rich and poor countries. Special attention should be paid to improve public transportation systems such as railways and subways. That would reduce the need to use cars and thus, alleviate traffic jams and reduce pollution. Work on the world's social infrastructure would focus on urban renewal, building low income housing and, in poor countries, improving fresh water supply and sanitation. In both rich and poor countries, the repair and renovation of existing social and economic infrastructure would also be major points of attention.

The fourth component of public investment would be to improve the working of government bureaucracies. Especially in poor countries, this would be a condition for successfully carrying out the other three components. The staff of government institutions should be motivated and trained, and brought to accept and apply the principles and ethics of public service. Particular attention should be paid to tax and law enforcement agencies, and to key public services such as education, health care, natural resource management and rural and urban development. Efficiency should be increased though phasing out excess staff and training those remaining. Where necessary, budgets for operational costs should be boosted. Especially in the poor countries, salaries and allowances should be raised to levels comparable to those in the private sector, to raise motivation and reduce the incentive for corruption.

The fifth public investment component would aim at research, especially in fields related to the first four components. Technical research on the substitution of non-renewable resources, recycling, and raising agricultural production in an environmentally sustainable manner would be of key importance. Studies on the more efficient use of scarce resources such as water and minerals would also be of interest. So would medical research and studies on the development of the mind, criminal behavior, and ways to improve learning and teaching.

Carrying out the above program would have a huge economic impact. Components one and three (environmental measures and infrastructural development) would generate an enormous upsurge in the building sector. That would create both blue collar jobs and employment for white collar technical workers, such as engineers. The second and fourth components would be major employment creators for white collar workers in the 'soft' sector, such as teachers and special educators, management specialists, medical personnel, psychologists and other social scientists. The fifth sector would generate jobs for both technical and social scientists.

In addition to the direct effect of job creation, the proposed program would also generate a huge demand for goods and services—most of which would be satisfied by the private sector. That would lead to more jobs as well as profits, which in turn, would further stimulate further economic growth and increase the demand for consumer goods and services. The latter, in turn, should raise demand for capital goods: the equipment needed to satisfy the new consumer demand. All this growth would lead to higher government revenues, giving governments the chance to further invest in sustainable development. Thus, the downward spiral caused by the growing gap between productivity and demand could be checked.

It's important to note that in time, investment in sustainable development would have similar or even stronger effects on lower and middle incomes than tax cuts. New employment opportunities and a slowing down of the competitive rat race would reduce the downward pressure on wages and thus, allow incomes to rise with productivity. Also, for both lower and middle income groups public services would not only become better but also cheaper, leaving more money to be spent on other things. Middle income groups might benefit the most as, seeing that public services would once more reach adequate levels, they could reduce today's growing dependency on the much more expensive private sector.

A bottom line in trade

A global program for sustainable development as described above would create huge numbers of jobs and allow lower and middle level incomes to rise. Still, these effects would probably not be enough to break the downward spiral of cut-throat international competition that today forces countries to sacrifice their environment and workers' rights. To counter this process, a 'bottom line' is needed: an international set of rules for establishing the minimum social and environmental norms to which business should comply.

The environmental bottom line should set international standards for pollution and the use of nonrenewable natural resources. This should prevent business from nations that now set the lowest or no standards from gaining a competitive edge. Thus, environmental dumping, that is, keeping down production costs at the cost of the environment, would no longer be possible.

Likewise, a social bottom line should make business from all nations comply with a set of standards for worker safety, benefits such as insurance and vacation, maximum working hours and minimum wages. The latter should vary from country to country, depending on overall productivity and the cost of living. That means that poorer countries could still maintain a labor cost advantage over the rich nations. As happens now, the rich countries should compensate by raising productivity through the use of high-tech production methods.

As we've seen in Chapter 1, today business can play off governments against each other so as to get the most favorable terms for investment. That leads not only to weakened social and environmental regulations, but also to governments trying to lure business with all sorts of tax breaks. The end result is that companies can operate paying only the barest minimum of taxes, or even none at all. At the same time, they enjoy direct and indirect subsidies in the form of cheap energy and the use of government built infrastructure such as roads, harbors and airports. Frequently, therefore, the cost of attracting foreign companies, especially for so-called 'free trade zones', outweigh the benefits. Thus, to ensure that business pays its fair share in taxes, the proposed bottom line would also have to include international agreements on corporate and other business taxes.

With the ground rules for international competition set, governments would no longer have to sacrifice the environment and well-being of their citizens to the scramble for investment capital. Likewise, with all companies having to comply with the same regulations, business would no longer compete at the cost of the environment and workers' rights. Instead, they would be forced to gain an advantage by making better products more efficiently. Thus, the downward spiral caused by global competition could be broken.

The main problem in implementing a bottom line would be that some nations would try to dodge it. In an open international market, this would mean unfair competition for business from complying countries. To prevent this, countries adhering to the norms should form a free trade block. Participating countries would freely trade amongst themselves, but would protect their private sector, through tariffs or import bans, from unfair competition from non-complying countries. The ultimate goal of such protective measures should, however, not be to protect national producers against foreign competition. Instead, it would be to push noncomplying countries into adopting and enforcing the bottom line, and so join the free-trade block.

The proposal to base free trade on a bottom line and especially to impose import barriers on non-complying nations, runs counter to the current drive for unconditional free trade. Mainstream economists and politicians will reject any proposal to tie trade to social and environmental restrictions. They will argue that doing so would endanger the economic growth that results from free trade. That, however, is doubtful. In 1992, the projected benefits of current free trade arrangements were estimated at some $120 billion a year, roughly 1/2% of the world's gross product. A more radical freeing of markets was figured to double that.[1] However, these projections do not consider the social, environmental and long term economic costs of social and environmental dumping. Nor do they account for the earlier mentioned effects of unchecked global competition: the vicious circle of stagnant demand, rising unemployment and declining real wages.

Another argument to defend unconditional free trade is that social and environmental regulations will make it more difficult for poor countries to compete in world markets. There's some truth to that. But this disadvantage could easily be compensated for through other measures. Current import barriers in the rich countries could be lowered, and the debts of the poor countries reduced. Also, poor countries should be helped, technically as well as financially, to comply with environmental norms. In any case, the problem of reduced competitiveness would be less than might appear at first sight. In export markets, producers from poor countries are more likely to compete with each other than with business from the rich nations. As the bottom line would apply to all poor countries, the new regulations would affect them equally. And in comparison with the rich countries, the poor countries would still retain a significant labor cost advantage.

Fostering local demand and production

The combined proposal of a bottom line in trade and a global investment program for sustainable development would mean a new strategy for economic development. Today's strategy, as we've seen, is to generate economic growth through increased international trade. The new strategy, on the other hand, would aim at fostering internal demand: through job creation generated by implementing a global program for sustainable development, and through pay raises resulting from a social bottom line.

Real economic development requires growth in both internal demand and the local capacity to efficiently produce high quality goods. Today, the problem in many poor nations is that this capacity cannot be developed. On the one hand, free trade allows cheap imports to push local, less efficient producers out of the market. Thus, countries in Africa and Latin America are today flooded by cheap products from Asia, notably China. On the other, because of low transportation costs and low or non-existent import barriers, it is much more attractive for business to export to a country than to set up shop there. Yet in less developed areas, the latter is what's needed. Companies should be coaxed to set up production in the market they want to serve, with local partners, using local labor and management and, whenever possible, locally produced raw materials.

To achieve this, foreign investment in less developed areas should be promoted by eliminating red tape and allowing the free flow of investment capital and profits. Also, the import of capital goods needed to set up production should be facilitated. On the other hand, import taxes should be levied temporarily to allow companies the time to set up production and conquer market share by pushing out imports. However, to ensure that locally producing companies would set and maintain sufficiently high standards of production, duties and tariffs should not aim to keep out imports altogether. Moreover, import barriers should be reduced gradually so as to force local business to remain competitive.

Local production should also be stimulated by promoting direct links between producers and consumers. The potential for eliminating distribution chains is particularly promising in agriculture and services. In hundreds of communities, especially in North America, Northern Europe and Australia, local groups are already engaged in community-supported agriculture, or CSA. As will be described in more detail in Chapter VIII, CSA involves a group of families purchasing their food directly from a local farmer. Payment takes place in advance; the produce is picked up at the farm or delivered to the consumer's home or central collection point once or twice a week.

Likewise, local production can be stimulated through Financial Micro-Initiatives. FMIs, which will be discussed in more detail in Chapter XIII, promote the local exchange of goods and services without the actual use of money. Instead, transactions are registered in the form of credits earned and spent. These credits can be considered as a kind of local money, used on a micro scale: hence the phrase FMI. FMIs are a particularly promising alternative for poor communities, where economic activity is hampered due to a lack of regular money.

CSA, FMIs and other cooperative efforts aimed at strengthening local economies all have social as well as economic benefits: in addition to fostering local economies, they build community ties and spirit. Moreover, as a rule they have a positive impact on the environment. CSAs promote diversified, ecologically sustainable forms of farming, in which care of the land is an integral part of agricultural production. Moreover, the local production of goods and services reduces transport needs as well as the, often unsustainable, exploitation of natural resources in other regions or countries.[2]

From speculation to investment in production

As we've seen in Chapter I, governments in rich as well as poor countries are deeply in debt. For the time being, the cost of debt servicing will increase

rather than diminish. Moreover, in the rich countries, the graying of populations will result in growing expenditure on health care and pensions. That
leaves even less money for investment in sustainable development than is the
case today.

The problem is not that there's no capital: as we've seen, trillions of dollars circulate in the world's capital markets. Only about 1% of the $1 trillion
that changes hands each day is used for the trade in goods and services, the
rest involves speculative transactions. This puts entire economies at the
mercy of a handful of money managers and speculators. Tapping into this
capital would therefore be doubly beneficial. On the one hand, it would
generate funds for the production of goods and services for sustainable development. On the other, it would weaken the stranglehold financial markets
now have over all but the largest economies.

One way to tap into these funds would be to tax all sales of stocks, bonds
and currencies. This could generate billions of dollars each year. At the same
time, it would make large capital transactions more expensive, which would
reduce speculation and the volatility of markets. Of course, taxing capital
transactions would meet with a clamor of objections from money managers
and economists. They would assert that such a tax would hinder trade and
prevent capital from flowing where it can be used in the most efficient way.
But a tax of, say, 0.5%, would not impede a transaction if the intended investment were really worth it. It would put a brake, however, on the mad
scramble for short term capital gains that marks trading today.

Although a tax on capital transactions would help curb the speculation
in international financial markets, it would not be enough to end it. Curb-
ing speculation requires going to where the money comes from: the
wealthy and institutional investors such as pension funds and insurance
companies. We've seen in Chapter 1 how since the 1980s, the rich have acquired huge wealth at the cost of the rest of the population. High time,
then, that they pay something back. Higher taxes on the wealthy would put
money that is now drawn into the international financial circuit at the disposal of the state, which should use it to finance programs for sustainable
development.

Mainstream economists and politicians will oppose raising taxes on the
rich. They'll claim that it will reduce investment, and therefore, hamper production and economic growth. That's nonsense. As we've seen, the rich increasingly use their newly acquired wealth for speculation rather than productive investment. The only growth this has created is in the financial sec-

tor. But society hardly needs even richer bankers and financial managers. What it does need is investment in sustainable development, and the kind of jobs, profits and growth such investment would generate.

Institutional investors—insurance companies, mutual funds, pension funds—are also major contributors to speculative investment. To meet future obligations (payment of insurance claims, interest on deposits, and pensions) and of course, to turn a tidy profit on their operations, they constantly search for the highest capital gains. In doing so, they pump hundreds of billions of dollars into the international financial circuit, driving up the rate of speculation. Their role could be reduced by shifting part of their tasks back to the state. More elaborate government pension plans, involving all citizens, would increase the premiums paid to the state while diminishing those paid into private pension schemes. Similarly, disability and health insurance, as well as insurance for damage caused by natural disasters, could be taken over partially or entirely by the state. The premiums paid would increase the capacity to invest in sustainable development; future obligations could be met by the revenues resulting from those investments.

To increase the government's role in providing pensions and insurance goes, again, against established dogma. Today's economists, politicians and opinion makers favor reducing the role of the state. Pension funds, health care, disability insurance and other forms of social security are increasingly 'privatized': delegated to the private sector. This is supposed to increase efficiency, especially in the management of assets. Because of this, the argument goes, the private sector will be better able to meet future obligations than the government.

This is doubtful at best. The track record of financial institutions in the 1980s has hardly been encouraging. True, institutional investors played a relatively minor role in the speculation and the crash that followed it. That, however, was at least partly due to the fact that pension funds and insurance companies were more subject to regulation. Since then, as financial markets have been liberalized further, part of these restrictions have disappeared. There is little reason to assume that, once they get the chance to play the game all-out, institutional investors will do a better job than banks. A greater role of the state in managing pensions and some forms of insurance would, therefore, be no more than prudent. In the short and medium term, yields of the capital involved could turn out to be somewhat lower. But this would be more than compensated for by the lesser chance of massive losses through speculation or other forms of high-risk investment. Thus, problems like the banking crises of the last decade, which cost tens of billions of taxpayer money to resolve, could be avoided.

Obviously, the wealthy and institutional investors would strongly oppose the above proposals. Still, in the end they might benefit even more than society at large. The proposed measures could help avert the financial collapse that will be unavoidable if the current rate of speculation continues. In addition to causing a global economic and financial crisis, this crash would ruin private as well as institutional investors. Better, then, to restructure before it is too late—even though some of the beneficiaries will have to be dragged in kicking and screaming.

The roles of private enterprise, the market and the state

The above proposed measures for sustainable development, fair trade and tapping into the international financial circuit require a stronger state. Today, talking about strengthening the state is taboo: one of the worst things one can say about politicians is that they favor a greater role of government. Instead, government should 'get off the backs' of citizens and, in the economic sphere, let the 'invisible hand of the market' do its work.

Yet to expect the private sector to plan, coordinate and carry out something resembling a program for sustainable development is foolish. Private enterprise strives for short and medium term profits. That's a goal that is fundamentally different from, and can be contrary to, the long term common good. Private enterprise reacts to demand: it satisfies the needs of those who can pay for it. The problem is that many needs in society are not backed by this ability. Sustainable development aims to satisfy all people's basic needs: at taking the measures to fight poverty, crime and environmental deterioration. Private enterprise will engage in sustainable development only if it's paid to supply the required goods and services. That means the initiative for sustainable development will have to come from elsewhere: from an entity concerned with the short, medium and long term common good. That entity is, and can only be, the state.

As said, the fact that the government plans and leads the drive for sustainable development does not mean the private sector is left out. On the contrary, private enterprise would be essential for producing the needed goods and services. Market forces, in the form of companies competing for contracts, should be used to ensure that this production would take place as efficiently as possible. Thus, the state, by converting the needs of society into demand, would orient part of the energies of the private sector to production for sustainable development.

Let's use an analogy. The private sector can be seen as a large herd of very well built, strong and smart animals, each with its own single-minded purpose: to eat as much as possible. If this herd is set free the animals will move in any direction, fighting among each other, damaging and in some cases destroying their environment. Therefore, the herd must be harnessed. It must be set on the right path and made to face the right direction. Its strength must be garnered to move a huge structure, society, situated in a delicate environment, in a specific direction: that of sustainable development.

Once the structure is moving along, the herd must be guided to follow the right path. It must be controlled and fed. The road over which it draws the structure must be prepared. All that is the role of the state. It must develop and maintain a good transport and communications system, and feed business with well-trained people and knowledge generated through scientific research. Through a Central Bank (in the u.s., the Federal Reserve System), it also supplies the private sector with that most important lubricant of business: money. Moreover, the state sets rules so that the single-minded pursuit of profit does not harm the environment, workers or consumers.

Business should not be afraid for a stronger role of government. Using another analogy, we can look at the state as both the coach and the referee of a game in which many players take part. In combining these roles, the state should set and enforce the rules needed to ensure that the game is played fairly, and that non-players don't get hurt. That is, the state should ensure free competition, and avoid that workers, consumers or the environment get hurt by companies breaking the rules. For people as well as companies, it's more fun, safer and more profitable to play a game when the rules are clear and apply to everybody. Especially smaller players will profit: it is only the strongest, most vicious players who gain in a free-for-all. Most companies, therefore, benefit from a strong state that is able to level the playing field for all contenders.

In fact, one of the prime beneficiaries of a state strong enough to set in motion a sustainable development program would be business. The above described program, especially the first and third components (the conversion to an ecologically sustainable economy and the improvement of the world's economic and social infrastructure), would offer huge opportunities. On the other hand, if something like the proposed program for sustainable development is not set in motion, increasingly large numbers of companies will fall prey to the growing gap between productivity and demand. In spite of laying off workers and capping the wages of those remaining, they may no longer be able to compete and will drop out of the treadmill. In the longer run, therefore, sustainable development, and the strong state required to set it in motion, are their best bet for survival.

Much of the drive for sustainable development would be aimed at the poor countries. There the needs are greatest, whereas demand is smallest. Rich countries should therefore assist poor countries in fostering sustainable development. For the rich countries' business sector, that would mean vast opportunities in engineering, construction and management.

Of course, the history of international business operating in poor countries is not without blemish. Yet for sustainable development, both poor and rich nations must garner the know-how and productive potential that international business can offer. To do so in the most effective way, and to ensure that the involved companies would comply strictly with national and international regulations, would require all nations to cooperate closely.

Chapter VII

ELIMINATING POVERTY

Human development: education and health care

In previous chapters we've seen how over the last fifteen years, the number of poor has grown and poverty has deepened. Even some economists are now beginning to see that free trade, lowering taxes, and responsible monetary policies are not enough to eliminate poverty. To their credit, a few are even advocating special measures to increase the poor's economic potential. Notably, they argue for better education and, to a lesser extent, health care. They are right: to fight poverty, the development of people's skills and, in the case of the destitute poor, improving people's health is essential.

The economic function of education is to increases people's capacity to make a decent living. This is complemented by a political function: education should strengthen people's capacity to evaluate their leaders critically. A well-educated population will not fall as easily for false promises, cheap rhetoric, half-truths and lies as a poorly educated one. It is less likely to accept corruption or support local power holders in exchange for minor handouts. Also, it will not stand for practices like vote buying, vote rigging and other ways of corrupting the democratic process. A good educational system, then, does not only lay the basis for economic development, but also for good government.

For people's well-being, good health is even more important than an adequate education. Giving all people, and especially the poor, adequate access to health care is therefore at least as important as giving them access to education. Good health is also crucial to making good use of the opportunities offered by education. To prevent the kind of physical and mental impairment that annually, in the poor countries, affects tens of millions of people, a well-developed system of primary health care is essential. Such a system should in the first instance aim at disease prevention, through vaccination programs, health monitoring—particularly of children and pregnant women —and information supply on such themes as nutrition and personal hygiene. Strong emphasis should be put on family planning, especially in countries with high birth rates. Curative services should aim at healing afflictions that can be treated locally, at low cost. More difficult cases should be forwarded to clinics and hospitals at the secondary and tertiary levels of the health care system.

Curative health care more often addresses symptoms than causes. As we've seen in Chapter II, most of the deaths among the destitute poor occur because people, especially children, don't have access to clean drinking water and sanitary facilities. In communities now lacking an adequate water supply, primary health care services should therefore be combined with the provision of clean drinking water.

Another key element for sustaining human health is, of course, adequate nutrition. Where needed, food programs should ensure to the extent possible that people are fed at least one nutritionally balanced meal a day. Groups that would qualify for such programs would be those unable to provide for themselves, such as (uncared-for) children, elderly people and severely disabled adults. For adults, strict criteria should be applied to be eligible for this form of food aid; whenever possible, the people involved should be incorporated in programs that would allow them to meet their own subsistence needs as soon as possible.

It is a collective obligation of any civilized society, then, to see to it that all its citizens live in a reasonable state of physical and mental health. The entity responsible for this collective obligation is the state. That does not imply that private enterprise or non-profit non-governmental organizations cannot be involved in satisfying these basic needs. Neither does it mean that those who can contribute to the cost of the required goods and services should receive them for free. Only the government, however, has the scope of operation, the legal means and the resources to ensure that all people enjoy an adequate standard of living, and that those who can contribute to achieving this actually do so.

Unfortunately, we're becoming less civilized. We've seen how in many poor countries, public education and health care are deteriorating rather then improving. The same goes for public services such as drinking water supply and sanitation. The causes were discussed in Chapter II: the debt problem, the economic policies and development strategies imposed by the international financial institutions, the spending priorities of local decision makers, and poorly functioning government bureaucracies. For the destitute poor, the failure of governments to satisfy people's most basic needs further decreases their chance to improve their situation. Eradicating poverty should, therefore, start with an all-out effort to provide every man, woman and child with that which is essential for human well-being and development: education, health care, drinking water, and adequate nutrition. Special attention should be given to the most vulnerable groups: children, women, and the elderly. The main priority should be to ensure that children receive the care and assistance needed to develop their full physical and mental potential. Although this will require a huge effort and, in many cases, a reorientation of economic, fiscal and developmental policies, it is by no means impossible. All it requires is, in rich as well as poor countries, the political will to foot the bill and get to work.

Start early—and finish

There is consensus among experts—medical researchers, psychologists, pedagogues, pediatricians—that the first few years of life are crucial for a person's development. Still, in rich as well poor countries, little attention is paid to early child development by people other than parents. Educators begin to exert their influence only when a child turns four or five, and enters into the formal education system. By that time, the foundations of a person's mental development have already been firmly established. That means that children from disadvantaged backgrounds start the educational process with a handicap. In extreme cases, the impairments may be such that the children involved will never be able to develop their full human potential.

It is impossible for the state to solve such problems completely. Yet much more could be done than is the case today. Future parents should be stimulated to follow courses on the early development of children; to ensure they actually would, failure to do so should be sanctioned by a reduction in child support benefits. The first months after birth, specialists should regularly assist parents in guiding and fostering the physical and mental development of their babies. After six months, parents should be encouraged to bring their babies, for a few hours a day, to special day care centers. There competent staff could, in an adapted, stimulating environment, foster the mental development of babies and toddlers. Such early guidance could go a long way in reducing the handicaps that children from disadvantaged backgrounds have today when entering the regular school system. This would also benefit other pupils, as the problem of poorly learning children keeping back the whole class and thereby lowering overall educational standards, would be diminished.

Guiding the development of children at as early an age as possible would have other advantages. Part time day care would give mothers more opportunities to work and would allow them more time for household chores and leisure. That would be especially important in poor countries, where work loads for women are often excessive. Increased well-being of mothers would contribute to parents paying more attention to their child's development, and reduce the chances of neglect or abuse. Also, assistance in child care from the earliest age on would allow the coaching of mothers in aspects such as nutrition, hygiene and stimulating the mental development of their children. Parents should therefore be encouraged to participate as much as possible in the day care system—which would have the additional advantage of cutting costs. Finally, the proposed system would allow closer health monitoring, which would allow for detection, at an early stage, of any signs of disease, nutritional problems or child abuse.

Thus, the first principle of eradicating poverty—and in general, for sustainable development—should be to start early. The second should be to have children finish their education. Education should be made compulsory not until a specific age, but until an educational career aimed at entry into the economy is completed. The phenomenon of drop-outs should be made a thing of the past. Students unable or unwilling to finish their training in a regular school should be sent to a special institution to do so. That would avoid the problem of students with a dislike for learning just sitting out their time in school, until they reach the age at which education is no longer compulsory. And of course, compelling them to finish would greatly improve their job prospects.

In most poor countries special measures would have to be taken to ensure that all children would actually go to school. Especially in very poor families, children of school age often play important roles in household chores, looking after younger siblings, doing agricultural work, and as income earners. Educational planning should take this into account by scheduling school hours and vacations accordingly. Simultaneously, the use of simple, cheap technology that would diminish or eliminate the need for child labor should be promoted. Special attention should also be given to technology to alleviate the tasks of poor women in the rural areas of poor countries, who today are highly dependent on help from their children.

Another key element in alleviating poverty, especially in poor countries with high illiteracy rates, would be adult education. Besides literacy and numeracy, this type of instruction should focus on teaching readily appli-

cable, practical knowledge. Particular attention should be paid to skills for locally relevant economic activities, such as small scale agriculture, trading and
crafts. Also, adult instruction as well as the higher grades of juvenile education should include courses in civics. These should make people familiar
with the basic principles and tasks of government as well as with the rights
and obligations of citizens. Points to be emphasized would be among others,
the functions of the nation state, the duties and responsibilities of elected officials, and human rights—including the right of each citizen to equal treatment and access to public services. Also, attention would have to be paid to
the principle of taxation, as the means to finance the services provided by the
state. In short, civic instruction should aim to create an understanding of
people's rights and duties in modern society—including the need to keep
tabs on their leaders and representatives at community, state and national
level.

Other important themes for adult education would be health and ecology.
Information on health should focus on, among others, ways to prepare a balanced diet with locally available ingredients, illness prevention, and family
planning. In ecology, the awareness about the interdependence between
people and their environment should be strengthened. Special attention
should be paid to pollution and other negative effects of human activity on
nature. In rural areas, this should tie in with a powerful effort to convert to
forms of agriculture in which natural resources, notably soils and water, are
used in a sustainable manner.

Job creation and access to means of production

By themselves, education, health care and assistance in improving living conditions are not enough to resolve the problem of poverty. The most that can
be expected is that these services would put people in a proper starting position to take part in the economy. To actually achieve such participation requires jobs and possibilities for self-employment.

One way to create jobs was already discussed in the previous chapter: a
sustainable development program. In the rich countries, public investment
in social and economic infrastructure and in sustainable energy use would
create large numbers of jobs for which relatively little schooling is needed. In
poor countries, land reclamation, erosion control, reforestation, and the
building of dams and reservoirs for water management would be important

employment creators. The same would hold for the construction of roads and bridges, water works and sanitary facilities.

As was already explained, carrying out such programs for sustainable development would stimulate local and regional economies directly and indirectly. Higher incomes would lead to increased demand for locally produced foodstuffs, clothing, and other basic consumer goods. That would create new jobs and also opportunities for the self-employed poor. Trade would pick up as the demand for non-locally produced goods would grow. Thus, the initial capital injection through programs aimed at sustainable development would set in motion a general process of economic development.

A complementary strategy to job creation would be to improve the access of the poor to the production factors they most sorely lack: land and capital. In the poor countries, as we've seen, a prime cause of rural poverty is that people do not possess agricultural land. Often, this is caused by very skewed land ownership; as was indicated in Chapter II for the case of Brazil, a small group of very large, very rich land owners possess most of the arable land. The poor work as day laborers, for dismally low wages, or as share croppers. In the latter case, the land rent is often so high (usually, a third of the harvest, sometimes as much as one half) that they remain with only the barest minimum for their own use.

To counter this, excessively large holdings should be redistributed. One way to achieve this would be through the introduction of a progressive land tax: a tax on land ownership the marginal rates of which would rise with the size of the holding. This would force large landowners to sell the land for which taxes would be higher than the profits obtained though productive activities. Such land could be bought by governments, to be redistributed among small farmers and the landless.

Almost by definition, capital is the scarcest production factor among the poor. In urban as well as rural areas, small scale entrepreneurs should get access to working capital in the form of low interest loans. Often, the amount of funding needed is minimal: enough to buy some raw materials or products to sell, possibly some tools. Providing such small loans is unattractive for regular commercial banks. Because of lack of collateral and therefore, the impossibility to repossess loans, the poor are considered a major credit risk. Moreover, the small amounts concerned make for high costs. Therefore, it would be necessary to supply the poor via non-profit credit agencies. These should attempt to minimize overhead costs by keeping their infrastructure and procedures as simple as possible: no expensive, luxuriously decorated offices in large cities, but mobile bank officers reaching out to customers in their own localities. The fact that such banking is very well possible is shown among others by the Grameen Bank of Bangla Desh. In the 1980s and early 1990s, this institution provided loans of no more than $200 at a relatively low annual interest rate of 16%. For 1993 it was reported that of all loans 93% had been repaid on time. That certainly compared favorably with the repayment rate of 35% obtained by the government development bank, which lends primarily to wealthier farmers and traders.

Housing

In the rich countries people with low incomes cannot as a rule afford to own their own homes. Unemployment, decreasing real wages, and cutbacks in social security and subsidies on low cost housing have worsened the situation, and led to growing rates of homelessness. No civilized society should accept that people are denied the basic human right to shelter. If people cannot provide for shelter themselves, because their wages are too low or because they cannot find employment, the state should do so. In many countries, it does. Public housing programs provide people with low rent apartments. In some countries, people with low incomes who pay more than a specified percentage of their income in rent receive rent subsidies.

Yet today, as part of the drive to cut budget deficits, all these support measures are being scaled back. Furthermore, these systems have a major problem: they do not allow poor people to own their own home. So what's the solution? Donating homes to the poor would be unfair to those with higher incomes. Especially people from middle income groups have often worked hard to obtain their own home, and have to continue to do so to pay off their mortgages. They would require some form of compensation too.

A fair solution would be to give every citizen a housing voucher, reflecting the value of basic accommodation for an individual. The holder could exchange this voucher for ownership of a standard dwelling. Two persons living together could pool their vouchers to obtain a house or apartment for a standard family: two adults and one or two children.

The voucher system should be supervised by the state. Also, the state would have to see to it that a sufficient number of basic housing units would be available to provide for all citizens opting for one. On top of this public housing system there would be a private real estate market. Citizens wanting to purchase a more luxurious—and more expensive—house or apartment in this sector should be able to use their voucher to do so. The government would pay, to the seller, an amount equivalent to the nominal value of the voucher. The owner of the voucher would pay the balance. Upon selling the dwelling, the state would reclaim the value of the voucher or, in case a new house would be bought, transfer it to this new unit. At no point should a citizen be allowed to turn the voucher into money. Thus, the voucher would represent a right to housing rather than a monetary value: the latter would apply only in relationship to the purchase of a home.

Obviously, the cost of housing vouchers would be huge. On the other hand, the proposed system would end all subsidies on rents, mortgages and other benefits for home owners. It would also be much simpler to apply than the mazes of subsidies, procedures and regulations that are the rule today, allowing for a significant downsizing of government bureaucracies. Social security benefits could be lowered with a proportion equivalent to the cost of basic housing. Taken together, these savings could finance a major part of the home voucher program.

Especially in the rich countries, the most important advantage of the voucher system would be its fairness. At present those with high incomes, and the more expensive houses that go with it, benefit greatly from deducting mortgage interest payments from their taxes. Those with lower incomes and cheaper housing benefit much less, and those with no housing of their own, not at all. Housing vouchers would end this inequity, giving each citizen equal treatment.

A final advantage of the voucher system would be that it would increase the poor's expendable income. Now, lower income groups often pay a disproportionate share of their income in rent. Owning their own home, without a mortgage (assuming they would settle for a basic dwelling) would leave them only with the cost of maintenance. The money thus saved could be spent on other things or for savings—both of which would be good for the economy.

For most poor countries a home voucher system would, for the time being, be too expensive. Still, there the poor should also be helped in obtaining housing that would meet minimum standards of safety and hygiene. Simple building materials could be disbursed and technical assistance given to help poor families build their own dwellings. In urban areas, pre-fabricated housing might be the more feasible solution. The design of such dwellings should be made in close cooperation with the beneficiaries, and where needed, adapted to local preferences and custom.

A subsistence income

Another measure to fight destitute poverty would be to provide those unable to work with a subsistence income—as is already the case in most rich countries. A minimum of social security in the poor countries would be important not only from a human and social point of view, but also from an economic one. Notably, it would raise consumer demand for basic goods and services that these groups desperately need, but today cannot afford. Social security should be focused on two categories of people: the elderly and mothers with children.

Many poor countries already have rudimentary pension systems for their elderly. Often, however, those who have never held salaried jobs are not covered. That leaves tens of millions of people out in the cold. Moreover, in many nations inflation has strongly decreased the real value of pensions. What is left is insufficient to purchase even the most basic necessities. Because of structural adjustment policies and budget deficits, there is little chance that governments will adjust these pensions to the real cost of living. Nor is it likely that pension systems will be created where they do not yet exist.

The justification for providing the elderly with pensions high enough to satisfy their most basic needs is, in the first instance, moral: it's immoral not to take care of elderly people who are too old and infirm to work. The moral argument gains in strength when one takes into account that many of today's lower class elderly, especially those from the former East Bloc, have made huge sacrifices during their lifetime to ensure a better future for their children. That this future is now less bright than was once expected is not their fault.

From an economic point of view, providing pensions to the elderly poor could be an effective way to stimulate demand and even provide capital for investment in small-scale productive activities. Where it is customary for the elderly to live with their offspring, pensions could also help satisfy the basic needs of other household members.

Like pensions, child support would help a very vulnerable group in society while stimulating local demand for basic goods and services. It would improve the possibilities for children to grow up into healthy adults, able to cope in and contribute to society. Also, it would help to alleviate the enormous burden of mothers who have to raise children in conditions of extreme deprivation.

As a rule, child support should be paid to mothers. Where possible and feasible, it could be paid in kind, to ensure to the extent possible that the

benefits would accrue to the children. Moreover, child support could contribute to strengthening the position of women versus husbands or other
male relatives who, in many societies, control cash incomes. What should be
avoided, however, is that child support would become a stimulus for having
many children. Therefore, payments should in principle be made for no
more than two children. Only in exceptional cases should support be given
for additional offspring. Rather, child support should be used to encourage
family planning by providing an incentive for temporary or permanent steri-
lization. For example, women with one or two children who would have
themselves sterilized could be given, on top of their normal support payments, a permanent bonus equivalent to the support for one child.

Child support should involve only small amounts of money. It should be
part of a general approach to development, which should include the already
proposed programs for education, health care, and employment creation.
Together, these components should largely satisfy the basic needs of mothers
and children. The idea of child support would be to complement these
measures, so as to give poor and low income mothers some more leeway in
satisfying the needs of their children.

Good government and effective aid

Setting up and maintaining adequate educational and health care systems require a well-functioning government and civil service. The same goes for the
effective management of natural resources, housing and sanitation programs,
and pension and child support funds. Unfortunately, as we've seen in the
first part of this book, one of the major obstacles to development is that in
most poor countries, the state does not function well. Many officials consider
that their position gives them license for self-enrichment. In the process,
they act not so much for as against the interests of the poor. Therefore, an
important step in eradicating poverty is public sector reform: in government
institutions, a new mentality and a new concept of public service should be
developed. Development assistance from the rich nations and international
institutions could help make the required changes. To do so, however, a
radical change in the ways aid is given is needed.

Today, as we saw in Chapter II, aid does not do what it's supposed to do:
help the poor. It's been said, not incorrectly, that development aid is the poor
from the rich countries helping the rich from the poor countries. To change

the situation around, aid should be channeled into activities that benefit the poor directly. Those are the ones mentioned in this chapter: education and training, health care, housing and sanitation, job creation linked to natural resource management, small scale credit, and pension and child support funds. At the same time, to ensure that these activities are carried out effectively, aid should be aimed at assisting governments in making their civil service more task- and client-oriented, efficient and effective. Since all these activities involve investments that, though paying off in the long term, will not yield immediate economic benefits, funding should be provided in the form of grants and interest-free loans.

Effective development assistance is only possible when donor and recipient agree on its goals. If there is no such agreement, development cooperation becomes impossible. Governments that prefer spending on their military over investing in education and health care, and that have regressive tax regimes and high levels of corruption, will not use aid to alleviate poverty. Therefore, they should not receive aid at all. To help the poor in these nations, aid could be given through well-established non-governmental organizations that dedicate themselves to the already mentioned activities.

For poor countries with governments more responsive to poverty alleviation, aid for these activities should be channeled through the state. Simultaneously, such countries should be assisted in the above mentioned public sector reform, through reorganization and training. Where needed, judicial, economic and political reform should also be supported. Progress in these fields would also open the way to larger scale economic aid and cooperation. This could take the form of trade privileges, fostering private investment through credit guarantees, and infrastructural development. The latter could be financed through low-interest loans or, in the case of projects or programs with a high productive potential, loans on commercial terms. Thus, aid would come to consist of a joint effort of rich and poor countries to fight poverty.

Some people would cry foul. Especially likely to protest would be the top layers of society who, as we've seen in Chapter II, have appropriated most of the aid up to this time. They will say that conditioning aid is an infringement on their country's sovereignty, a return to the days of colonialism. They'll claim that, considering their imperialist history, the rich countries have an obligation to aid the poor countries, but have no right to tell those countries how that money should be used.

That is nonsense. Lower and middle income taxpayers in the rich countries have less of a debt to the poor countries than the political and economic leaders of those countries themselves. However, the citizens of the rich countries do have a moral obligation to help the poor. When they meet that obligation, they have every right to insist that their contribution benefits those for whom it is intended. Aid should therefore not be seen as countries helping countries, but people helping people. For practical purposes, and to have a lasting impact, aid will have to be channeled primarily, though not exclusively, via the state. Aid thus becomes a matter of governments of rich countries assisting those of poor countries in improving the situation of the poor. If the governments of poor countries do not use aid for that purpose, it should be stopped. To the extent possible, the donor government should then channel its aid via non-governmental organizations. It should be taken into account, though, that although this type of assistance can be important to alleviate the poor's immediate plight, it is unlikely to lead to genuine, long term improvements in their situation. For real development, a well-functioning, effective government is indispensable. Taxpayers from countries giving aid have therefore every right to demand, via their government, that governments of poor countries put their house in order, so that their money really benefits those for whom it is intended.

Chapter VIII

MANAGING THE ENVIRONMENT

Minimizing pollution

We saw in Chapter III that industry and agriculture use thousands of potentially toxic substances. Little or nothing is known of the effects of most of these materials on human health and the environment. In this situation, the only wise course is to take as few chances as possible. Pollution control should therefore aim to minimize emissions of all potentially harmful materials as much as technically possible.

This is a reversal of the current approach to pollution. Today, no action is taken unless it has been decisively proven that a substance causes harm. The risk of this approach is, of course, that by the time the proof is there it may already be too late: irreparable damage to people's health, the environment, or both may have taken place already. A good example is the case of the CFCs that affect the ozone layer: even though measures have now been taken to stop their production, the quantities already released will continue to do damage for decades to come.

Preventing pollution to the extent possible also makes economic sense. Undoing pollution, if possible at all, is terribly expensive, as the clean-up of toxic dumps and contaminated soil has shown. Avoiding pollution is therefore a lucrative investment, certain to generate huge savings in the future.

Of course, the minimization principle should be treated with some flexibility. Scarce funds, technical expertise, and production capacity for pollution control equipment limit the extent to which it could be put into practice. Priority should therefore be given to those forms of pollution control that would yield the greatest benefits at the lowest cost. Take, for example, the industrial pollutant sulfur dioxide. Eliminating the first 80% of this substance from industrial and vehicle emissions is quite affordable. The cost of cleaning the remaining 20%, however, rises exponentially. For nitrogen oxides, the turning point lies at 70%.[1] It would therefore be sensible to start out with the easy-to-eliminate proportions. The remaining contamination would be accepted temporarily, until new technology would lower the cost of its elimination. In the meantime, the funds saved could be invested in forms of pollution control that would have a greater impact for less money.

New ways of growth

We've seen in Chapter III that a prime problem in pollution control is that gains in reducing contamination per unit of waste are offset by increases in the amount of waste produced. This, and the finiteness of natural resources, has led some people to call for a halt to growth. To stop growth today is, however, unlikely to be popular with the many people who have not yet benefitted from economic development. Moreover, most of those who have profited from economic growth show little willingness to forego further benefits. Thus, apart from a small group of hard core environmentalists, there is little inclination to exchange growth for sustainability.

The way to resolve the dilemma between growth and sustainability is to change the character of growth. Economic growth should no longer be based on activities that increase pollution and the consumption of finite resources, but on activities that do the opposite. Pollution control, recycling, and renewable energy generation will create jobs, profits and thus, economic growth. But it will do so in ways that help achieve sustainability.

Economic growth, then, does not necessarily have to mean increased pollution and consumption of natural resources. This statement can also be reversed: pollution is not a necessary result of growth. Instead, in many cases it is a sign of inefficiency and indifference.[2] What is needed is a new approach to production, in which the starting point should not only be to maximize profits, but also to produce as few harmful emissions and use as few finite raw materials as possible.

To bring this about, two types of measures are needed. One is to ban the use of dangerous materials for which less harmful alternatives are available. Some examples already exist: in most rich countries the insecticide DDT has been prohibited, whereas worldwide, the CFCs that affect the ozone layer are being phased out. Overall, however, bans on dangerous chemicals are exceptions rather than the rule. The companies that produce them have huge interests in continuing their production and sale, and effectively lobby against prohibition. The users of these substances, especially the farmers and industries that use them as inputs in the production process, favor them because often the alternatives are more expensive. Still, a ban is the only way out. If alternatives are not readily available, a gradual phasing out will allow producers time to adapt their production process. A smooth transition can be aided by stimulating research into alternatives and, in exceptional cases, by subsidizing the latter's use.

For less harmful materials, including most non-renewable energy sources such as oil and coal, lesser usage and substitution should be stimulated through financial incentives. If the price for finite and polluting materials is raised, producers and consumers will use them more economically. Also, price rises stimulate the development and use of alternatives, and encourage re-use and recycling. The latter two practices have a double advantage: emissions are reduced and the need for new raw materials is diminished.

The way to raise prices is through taxation. That's not only practical, but also a matter of principle. The practical aspect, as said, is that the higher cost that results from taxation will stimulate a more economical use. The principle is that pollution and the use of non-renewable energy should carry a cost. After all, pollution affects soil, land and water, which should be considered as public resources. Polluters should compensate for that by paying the public, and a tax is the logical way to do so. Similarly, non-renewable natural resources should be considered as public property. At some point in the future, they will run out and will have to be replaced. A tax should be seen as a down-payment for the cost of that substitution. As such, it would be comparable to the depreciation costs calculated for machinery or buildings.

Most economists argue against environmental taxes. They will raise costs of production which, according to their models, costs jobs and reduces economic growth. Since natural resources are there for the taking, why pay more than is needed to cover the cost of their extraction? Better to let the market do its work, and avoid any government meddling in price setting. The problem is, however, that the market does not take account of future scarcity. Market prices of raw materials are determined by the supply and demand of the day. Traders are notoriously short-sighted: the longer term perspective of buyers and sellers does not reach further than a year, at the most. Nobody will purchase oil now to sell it at a profit when it is expected to become scarce, in a century or so.

Similarly, markets do not take account of the cost of environmental pollution. That's because those causing it don't pay for it. Air polluters do not pay for damage to forests or buildings, and water polluters do not pay the cost of replacing dead or contaminated fish and of making polluted water drinkable.

Other groups in society, and the public at large do. But since they're not part of the production chain, the cost to them is not reflected in the price of manufacturing.

The strongest argument economists have against environmental taxes is that, as said, they will raise prices for most goods and services. That will reduce sales and profits, cost jobs and depress economic growth. There's some truth to that. On the other hand, environmental taxes would stimulate private enterprise to invest in energy saving, pollution control and renewable energy generation. That would create business opportunities for companies working in these fields—and thus, jobs, profits and growth. Environmental tax revenues could be used to subsidize the conversion to a more sustainable use of raw materials. Also, the proceeds from environmental taxes could be used to lower the costs for public services such as education, health care and public transport. Income taxes could be lowered, and programs such as the home voucher program proposed in Chapter VII could be financed. That means that although environmental taxes might cause price rises for products manufactured in unsustainable ways, this would be compensated for by a rise in disposable income. Environmental taxes would therefore result not so much in economic contraction as in economic restructuring.

Environmental taxes should also serve to change consumer behavior. Nonsustainably produced goods and services would have to become more expensive in comparison to more environmentally friendly ones. The cost of the latter could also be lowered through subsidies. For example, the cost of driving private motor vehicles could be raised, and that of public transportation lowered. Short distance air travel could be made more expensive, railway transport cheaper. Energy consuming activities such as motorcycle, car or boat races could be taxed, whereas entrance costs to museums could be subsidized.

Of course, the effects of environmental taxes on economic growth depend strongly on the way growth is calculated. Without accounting for the cost of pollution and the future scarcity of finite natural resources, environmental taxes might indeed, initially, slow down economic growth, due to the required restructuring of the economy. Yet if environmental costs are included in production costs, environmental taxes would be certain to foster both short term and long term growth. The point is that to allow economic growth to continue in the future, allowances must be made now. The longer we wait with making these investments, the more it will cost us later.

Banning or taxing dangerous substances would be most effective if applied worldwide. They would constitute the 'environmental bottom line' suggested in Chapter VI, which would prevent business from countries not enforcing basic environmental norms from competing unfairly with business from countries that would. Obviously, as long as the bottom line would not be implemented worldwide, unfair competition would remain possible. Moreover, companies from complying countries could move their operations to non-complying countries. To counter this, governments could subsidize the switch to environmentally sustainable production. This could, as was already suggested, be financed from the proceeds of environmental taxes. Also, import bans or tariffs could be instituted on products from non-complying countries. To ensure fair competition, these should be at least equivalent to the degree with which the bans and taxes would raise production costs in complying countries.

A more general solution to the problem of compliance would be the suggested formation of a free trade bloc of nations applying the norms. An independent international organization would monitor compliance, and determine the height and character of trade barriers against products from non-complying, non-member nations. Also, the organization could be equipped to help both member and non-member nations enforce the standards. It should promote and, where needed, coordinate research on new technology for pollution control and the search for substitutes for dangerous substances. It could do that by providing funding to research institutes, universities and business. In exchange, it should be allowed a say in licensing the resulting technology worldwide, through joint ventures and other forms of cooperation between business.

Reducing garbage

In addition to the harmful emissions generated by industrial and agricultural production, there is the problem of the ever growing amounts of non-toxic refuse. The quantities involved are such that disposal has become a problem, particularly in densely populated areas. Moreover, non-renewable materials which will someday become scarce are thrown out with all his garbage.

One way to alleviate this problem is to improve the quality and serviceability of products. Repair should be favored over replacing, and quality standards should be set not only for durability, but also for serviceability. Currently, too many products have to be discarded because a spare part that costs only a few percent of the total price cannot be obtained or installed, or because it is too expensive to do so. Instead, products should be designed and constructed so that they are easily repairable—preferably by the consumer.

The amount of garbage could also be reduced by limiting the use of goods that are used only once, such as most packaging materials and throw-away consumer articles. For this, financial incentives would be important. Raising the price of disposal and charging according to the quantity of garbage produced would let producers and consumers take a closer look at alternatives for disposal, such as recycling. To do so cost-effectively, garbage would have to be sorted at an early stage. Garbage collection services should therefore encourage the separation of different forms of refuse—such as organic material (to be used as compost), paper, glass, metals and plastics. Adequate containers should be supplied, and reductions in collection fees offered to those who use them conscientiously. Initiatives to recycle could, where necessary, be encouraged through subsidies and tax breaks. Fortunately, in the u.s. and Northern Europe, many such measures taken at the local level are already in effect. However, only rarely have they been translated into national policy, as a result of which most communities and nations still continue their wasteful ways.

Consumer organizations could play an important role in raising public awareness of the garbage problem. They could issue seals for higher quality and better serviceable products, and encourage consumers to buy those rather than cheaper, poor quality alternatives. They could push business to recycle their waste products, and consumers to use recyclable instead of throw-away products. Also, they could influence retailers by recommending consumers to buy only at stores that sell durable, repairable and recyclable products.

Energy saving

Oil, gas and coal are burned for energy. Therefore, you can't recycle them. Yet as we've seen, we keep on using, even squandering these raw materials as if they were in infinite supply. Apart from future scarcity, there is a strong argument to be made for not using oil for energy generation at all since, as we've seen, burning oil produces carbon dioxide, the main Greenhouse gas.

Obviously, it is not possible to stop the use of oil for fuel from one day to another. Still, its future scarcity and the pollution caused by its burning should lead to a major effort to replace it as soon and as completely as possible with renewable energy: solar, wind, hydropower, earth warmth, biomass. That conversion will take time. In the meantime, oil use should be limited as much as possible by energy saving, and by substitution with gas and coal.

Much can be achieved by increasing energy efficiency. The u.s., by far the world's largest user of energy, has enormous potential in this field. Using energy saving technology that is already available, the u.s. could produce everything it does now against the same or lower costs. If it would, global oil consumption could be reduced by 14%, coal use by 10%, and the use of gas by 15%. Taken together, the rich countries could, without affecting production or sacrificing economic growth, realize energy savings of up to 30%. This would not involve major investments, and be economically feasible even at today's low energy prices.[3]

With a greater effort, even more can be achieved. Studies have shown that until 2020, industrial countries could reduce their energy use by at least half without a detrimental effect on their economies.[4] Even for a relatively energy-efficient country like Holland, a 1994 study shows that over the coming decades, a reduction in energy use of as much as 80% would very well be possible.[5]

For those countries where energy saving is still in its infancy, the potential is even greater. Huge savings can be achieved in the former East Bloc and in developing countries such as China, India and Brazil. In Russia, oil supplies have always been, and still are, abundant, whereas exploitation costs are relatively low. Consequently, there has been little incentive for increasing energy efficiency. As a result, manufacturing now requires three times as much energy as in the rich countries. Worse, antiquated oil pumping facilities and transport systems, with old, poorly maintained and leaking pipes, cause huge losses and widespread damage to the environment.

Even at today's low prices for nonrenewable energy, increasing energy efficiency is good business. In international markets, it can give companies an important competitive advantage. One reason German companies can still compete with u.s. industry, in spite of higher wages and taxes, is that German industry uses only half as much energy to produce the same amount of goods. Similarly, energy saving gives Japanese companies, also twice as energy-efficient as u.s. ones, a 5% price advantage in international markets.[6]

At world level, studies estimate that every $1 invested in improving energy efficiency can lead to savings of $5 in the supply of energy. Thus, over a period of 35 years, $350 billion invested in energy saving could eliminate the need for $1.75 trillion worth of power plants.[7] Developing nations, with their rapidly growing energy needs and low efficiency, could save hundreds of billions of dollars.

What is needed, then, is to launch a large-scale global effort to raise energy efficiency. As with pollution, changes in behavior should be brought about through directives and incentives. Directives should make business and consumers adopt the most energy-efficient option that is available at an acceptable price. For example, in colder climates building regulations should see to it that energy use is minimized by the use of double glass windows, insulation, and solar energy for (water) heating. In existing buildings, home owners and businesses should be obliged to bring these up to minimum standards for energy efficiency. Where need be, financial support should be given in the form of subsidies.

As for incentives, raising the price of non-renewable energy through an energy tax would stimulate people and business to use energy more economically and, where possible, replace it with renewable sources. It would also push the private sector to further develop renewable energy technology. The potential is enormous. Solar, wind and geothermal energy (earth warmth) are sufficiently abundant to satisfy all the world's electricity needs hundreds of times over. Especially solar energy is plentiful: the earth receives 2500 times as much as is needed to satisfy today's energy needs. All u.s. power needs could be met with solar power plants spread over some 60,000 square kilometers, or by fully exploiting the wind power potential of just three states — North Dakota, South Dakota and Texas.[8] Even today, renewable energy could easily meet 28% of u.s. energy needs—up from the current 2 to 3%.

Where the direct use of solar or wind energy is not an option, hydrogen should be used. Hydrogen can be produced from water with solar power. In fuel cells, it combines with oxygen to generate electricity. Since fuel cells can do that efficiently, cleanly and on a small scale, they offer enormous potential for propulsion. In Germany, hundreds of millions of Marks are already spent on research to develop hydrogen powered cars and airplanes. Economical, compact versions for cars and trucks could begin to make an appearance between 2000 and 2010.[9]

The burning of hydrogen produces only water—no carbon dioxide or other pollutants. Therefore, it would be the fuel of choice in the effort to contain the Greenhouse effect. In principle, the potential for using hydrogen as a source of energy is almost unlimited. With the solar energy of just three percent of the world's desert surface, enough hydrogen could be produced to substitute all the oil and gas used today.

The problem in converting to renewable energy use, then, is not so much technical as economic. The main problem, as said, is that the price of non-renewable energy is based only on present supply and demand. If future scarcity and environmental damage were taken into account, the prices of oil, gas and coal would rise significantly. That would make substitution with nonrenewable energy economically feasible. Unfortunately, an environmental tax reflecting the real cost of the use of non-renewable energy is not popular, least of all in the energy guzzling u.s. The needed changes will come about only if people, realizing their responsibility to future generations, exert massive public pressure on politicians to take the required measures.

Natural ecosystems

Even more urgent than economizing our use of non-renewable energy is the conservation of the world's natural ecosystems. Our supplies of oil will still last us close to a century. However, as things are going now, we'll run out of rain forest and wetlands within a few decades. Moreover, technological development will allow us to supplant oil as an energy source or raw material. Ecosystems such as rain forests and wet lands, however, are impossible to replace. Lastly, whereas oil does not directly sustain life, the earth's ecosystems produce two of its most basic building blocks: fresh water and oxygen.

A major step in the preservation of ecosystems is to address the problem of rural poverty in the poor countries. Two-thirds of the area of rain forest that disappears each year is lost to poor people clearing land to cultivate crops. For mountain forests, this proportion may be higher still. One measure to combat rural poverty was already discussed: the progressive land tax. Through this tax, poor landless families could be provided with a plot of their own in already cleared lands. Another option is to help people use the marketable resources of natural areas in more sustainable ways. Logging could be selective, meaning that only useful trees would be felled. That would give the rest of the system the chance to recuperate. Even more promising is the harvest of natural products, such as fruits, nuts, rubber and medicinal plants. It has been estimated for the Amazon forest that over a fifty year period, such harvesting would yield seven to nine times more income than logging. And that's not counting the possible royalties from patented medicines based on forest ingredients. At present, the turnover in such medicines is close to $100 billion each year.[10]

Another major threat to forests is mining. It has been estimated that some areas of the Amazonian rain forest could yield close to U.S. $600,000 per hectare in minerals. With such economic interests at stake, conservation of every single hectare of untouched area becomes difficult indeed. The wiser policy might be to aim for forms of mining that limit environmental damage to a minimum, and allow forest regeneration. International cooperation in developing and implementing such systems could contribute to minimizing environmental damage and maximizing the proceeds from exploitation.

Besides protecting natural areas, attention should be paid to reforestation. Replanting forests would help protect soils and watersheds, and regulate local climates. Erosion prevention would prevent the fouling up of rivers and the sedimentation of waterways and reservoirs. If properly managed, the wood from older forests could be harvested selectively for fuel and construction. Thus, reforestation and forest management would create new employment opportunities for the rural poor, and keep them from moving into and destroying natural areas.

Agriculture, water and soil management

As we've seen in Chapter III, modern agriculture is highly polluting and dependent on nonrenewable energy. Especially in poor countries, a wide range of toxic products cause illness and death, and threaten long term human health. Heavy machinery and chemicals destroy soils whereas in irrigated areas, unsound management leads to the waste of water and the salinization of soils.

At the same time, small scale agriculture in poor countries, on land unfit for agriculture, leads to erosion. Without natural or artificial fertilizers, yields decline. As a result, people are forced to look for new land, often in natural areas, or try their luck in the city.

The deterioration of agricultural land and the wastage of fresh water should be countered, as suggested in Chapter VI, by creating a global infrastructure for water management and a worldwide program for soil protection, land improvement and land reclamation. Moreover, to avoid the renewed deterioration of agricultural land and protect still productive soils, the above two forms of unsustainable agriculture should be supplanted by forms that pair high levels of production with the conservation of soil, water, and plant nutrients. That means that to the extent possible, nutrients that are taken out of the soil during the growing cycle are returned to it. Among others, that is achieved by applying animal manure, crop residues and organic refuse from the cities, converted into compost. Instead of using toxic pesticides, farmers could protect their crops through more natural methods. A wide array of methods is available: from the use of different crop varieties to crop rotation, the mixing of different crops and the release of natural enemies of insects.

It is still an open question if chemical inputs should be abolished altogether. At present, yields obtained by farmers who practice organic or ecological agriculture and therefore, do not use any chemicals, are as a rule still considerably lower than those on conventional farms. Moreover, organic agriculture has proven its potential mostly in good production conditions, that is, on fertile soils in a favorable climate. In less favored areas the lesser availability of plant nutrients and higher susceptibility to pests and diseases make for a greater dependence on chemical inputs. Yet research could well lead to the closing of this gap. A study by the U.S. Department of Agriculture shows that at least in the U.S., organic farming is economically viable even today.[11] Although it requires more human labor, it takes less energy per unit of product. That makes it an interesting alternative for a future in which the cost of energy is likely to rise.

However, even if farmers do not turn entirely organic they can, in most cases, produce in much more sustainable ways. They should be stimulated to do so in the way already described: through bans and incentives. The most harmful chemicals and practices should be prohibited; financial stimuli should encourage farmers to change practices that cause damage to the environment. One positive incentive would be to provide farmers willing to convert to sustainable farming with free or subsidized technical assistance. Also, subsidies could be given for investments in equipment and infrastructural works, such as improved irrigation systems. At the same time, higher prices for non-sustainable inputs, notably chemical fertilizers and pesticides, would encourage farmers to economize on their use and look for alternatives.

Savings in input use could also be achieved by locating agricultural activities in the areas best suited for them. A 1992 report of the Dutch Scientific Council for Government Policy gives an impression of the potential of this approach. Referring to the European Community as a whole it estimated that, by limiting cultivation to the most suitable soils and climates, fertilizer use could be reduced by almost 80% and pesticide applications by 95%.

The drive for a more ecologically sustainable agriculture should be combined with an approach to resolve the social problems in the sector. As we've seen in Chapter I, a much smaller number of farm enterprises than exists today could satisfy all of the world's demand for agricultural products. If present trends continue, all but the largest, most technically advanced producers will go out of business. The result will be huge economic and social problems for millions of farm families, who will be hard put to find work elsewhere in the economy.

Progressive land taxes, land management fees and community supported agriculture

The agricultural problem, then, is not so much an economic as a social and environmental issue. Especially in the rich countries, the priority should not be to increase efficiency even further—which would only create even larger surpluses—but to allow people to make a living off the land. This can be achieved with two complementary concepts: land management fees, and the already mentioned progressive land taxes.

In Chapter VII, the progressive land tax was discussed as a way to provide landless farmers in poor countries with their own land. In rich countries also a progressive land tax could be installed to avoid the concentration of land among agribusiness and wealthy land owners. That would leave more land for today's farm families, allowing those who would want to continue farming to do so. Also, non-farm families could acquire land to use it as a source of income.

The second concept, the land management fee, involves payment for the adequate, ecologically sustainable management of land. The principle underlying the fee is that all land where human activity has disrupted the natural ecosystem needs to be managed. Even though land may be privately owned, it is in the final instance a public resource—as are air and water. People who manage this public resource adequately should be compensated by the community, represented by the state, for doing so.

The height of the fees would depend on the costs of sustainable management. If costs are high, higher fees are in order than when they're low. The fees would provide a basic income for land owners and their families—including farmers. Additional income could be obtained through farming, forestry, tourism, or any other activity that could be carried out in an ecologically sustainable manner. As is already the case in the rich countries today, these activities should fit into local, regional and national land use plans.

For farmers, the system of land management fees would mean that they would be agricultural producers as well as paid caretakers of natural resources. They could gain additional income from forestry and tourism. Price supports for agricultural products would disappear, and market forces would again be the mechanism that would create a balance between supply and demand. Yet the basic income provided by the fees would avoid the social problems now caused by the workings of the market.

Although land management fees would help, it would still leave farmers wide open to the volatility of the market. This dependency could be diminished by establishing direct links between producers and consumers, through community-supported agriculture, CSA. Many forms of CSA have already sprung up in North America and Northern Europe, the basic principle being that farmers contract the sale of their produce directly with families in the community. By paying a fixed price in advance the consumer-participants assume part of the risks of price fluctuations and crop failures. In exchange for this risk sharing, consumer-participants receive a regular supply of varying combinations of high quality vegetables, herbs, fruits, flowers and dairy products, produced without chemical inputs in environmentally sustainable ways.[12]

In addition to the obvious health benefits, CSA offer the additional environmental advantage of minimal transport needs. Most of the agricultural produce that can be found in today's supermarkets travels hundreds or even thousands of kilometers before it reaches the consumer. The savings that can be obtained with CSA, both in non-renewable energy and transport costs, are therefore substantial.

Costs and benefits

The cost of land management fees would be considerable, and CSA would also be likely to raise the price of food. Today's agricultural support programs, however, are also expensive. In the early 1990s, the U.S. spent some $35 billion each year on farm subsidies, the European Community about $60 billion. Most of this support was given in the form of price subsidies; also, to avoid overproduction, farmers were paid to keep land out of production. Obviously, large producers and land owners benefit the most from such measures. Consequently, in 1990, 80% of the European Community sub-sidies went to the wealthiest 20% of farmers.[13] In the U.S., this figure was about 70%—with the richest 1% of farmers receiving as much as 30%.[14] A combination of land management fees and progressive land taxes, on the other hand, would put state support where it is needed: with the small family farm.

Economists are likely to argue that the above proposed measures would decrease efficiency. Land management fees would keep inefficient farmers in business, and the higher prices of environment-friendly produced agricul-tural products would reduce spending in the other sectors of the economy. That would dampen economic growth. Still, new technology for sustainable agriculture could help raise yields and lower production costs. The potential could well be considerable: at present, only a minute proportion of agricul-tural research spending goes to organic agriculture. A larger input should lead to interesting results—although, because of the local character and diversity of organic agriculture, not as spectacular as those obtained in the 'Green Revolution' caused by industrial agriculture.

Perhaps the most important argument in favor of organic agriculture is that, due to the much greater diversity in crops and crop varieties, it would enhance global food security. On the one hand, diversity reduces the risk of the massive crop failures that could occur in industrial agriculture, due to a major pest overcoming the resistance of widely used crop varieties while it-self acquiring resistance to pesticides. On the other, the much broader genetic base of crops and crop varieties would increase possibilities for plant scientists to develop new strains with resistance to such major pests.

All in all, then, even if consumer prices for agricultural produce would rise somewhat, it would be worth it. In exchange, food security would be in-creased and rural employment opportunities expanded. Moreover, environ-mental pollution would be reduced, farm environments would become more attractive, and consumers would get better quality and healthier products.

Chapter IX

REDUCING CRIME

Solicited crime: from prohibition to regulation

In Chapter IV we looked at several forms of crime. *Solicited crime* satisfies a demand; supplier and consumer engage in it voluntarily. Examples are the sale and use of drugs, gambling, and (unforced) prostitution. *Unsolicited crime* makes unwilling victims, and can take two forms. *Direct crime*, such as robbery, rape, and murder, affects the victim directly. *Indirect crime* is not aimed at and does not harm a particular person, but affects society as a whole. Examples are corruption, tax evasion and the illegal dumping of toxic waste.

If asked what sort of crime causes the most harm to society, most people would probably answer 'drugs'. Drug production, trade and consumption are solicited crimes. It is important to note, however, that by themselves, these activities cause relatively little damage to society: the number of deaths caused by the use of hard drugs such as heroin and cocaine is only a fraction of that caused by tobacco or alcohol. The problem is not so much the solicited crime itself as the unsolicited crime that accompanies it. Legitimate business people will not engage in satisfying the demand for illegal goods and services: because it's illegal, only criminals will. Such people don't stick to the rules that govern regular economic competition. Conflicts are resolved through violence, and sales are furthered by every illegal means available.

Of course, it would be great if in one big sweep, both the solicited crime and the unsolicited crime that accompanies it could be eliminated. That has been tried throughout history, all over the world. It has never worked. The prohibition and persecution of 'vices' does not eliminate demand. Its only effect is to drive production, trade and consumption underground where, unregulated and out of control, it fosters unsolicited crime. Apart from drugs, a clear example in recent history is that of the U.S. in the 1930s, when in the period of 'Prohibition', the production, distribution and consumption of alcohol was outlawed. The continuing demand for alcoholic drinks created enormous opportunities for organized crime. Criminal activity included not only large-scale solicited crime, in the form of the illegal production and distribution of alcohol, but also unsolicited crime. Turf wars between gangs led to widespread violence, including murder. The enormous sums of money going around corrupted the authorities: policemen, judges and politicians joined the payrolls of organized crime. What became a cancer in society was not the consumption of alcohol, but the side effects of its prohibition.

Replacing the word alcohol for drugs, the above applies word for word to the situation today. What makes things worse is that drugs are even more difficult to control than alcohol in the time of Prohibition. Drugs are less voluminous than alcohol, and therefore easier to smuggle. Many of the criminal organizations involved in production and trade are based outside consumer countries, making prosecution much harder. And today's crime cartels are even more vicious than the gangs that ruled at the time of Prohibition.

As was the case with alcohol in the 1930s, then, it is obvious that the drug problem cannot be solved through prohibition. In the u.s., the much ballyhooed 'War on drugs' has failed utterly; even the involvement of the military has hardly made a dent in the inflow of drugs into the country. Internationally, the social, economic and political problems caused by drug related crime continue to grow. In the rich countries, neighborhoods are terrorized by gangs who base their power on the drug trade. In producing countries, drug money has corrupted officials, including the military, up to the highest levels.

Prohibition, then, doesn't work. That brings us to a second option: legalization and regulation. It was the option chosen sixty years ago by the political leadership of the United States: after thirteen years, Prohibition came to an end. Alcohol production, distribution and consumption became legal, alcohol-related crime disappeared, and taxes on production, distribution and sales brought in government revenues. That's the practical argument for legalization. There is, however, also a moral argument. The starting point is that every adult individual should have freedom of choice regarding matters that affect himself. If one recognizes this basic human right, the state has no moral right to interfere in an individual's decision to use drugs. It's ironic that in the u.s., where individual freedom is most ardently hallowed and government intervention in private lives condemned, the opposition to free choice in a private matter such as drug use is strongest.

Opponents of legalization clamor that condoning the use of drugs will corrupt society in general, and youths in particular. Such people confuse legalization with deregulation. It is true that especially the continued use of hard drugs can harm people's well-being. The same, incidentally, goes for alcohol, cigarettes and fatty foods. Still, the decision to engage in such vices remains a personal responsibility. The state has the task to regulate production, distribution and consumption in such a way that the chance of damaging side effects, for consumers as well as non-consumers, is minimized. In this respect, treatment of drugs should be no different than that of any other potentially harmful commodity.

The most important element of regulation would be to limit the option of drug use to people who have reached an age where a considered decision can be made. That age should be put at eighteen years—the voting age in most countries. If people are old enough to choose who should govern them, they should be considered old enough to make decisions on the use of drugs. To anyone younger than eighteen, production, distribution and consumption should be strictly off limits. The corresponding laws should be enforced rigorously, and offenders punished severely—particularly if they're profit-motivated adults.

The second element of regulation should be to discourage consumption as much as possible. All forms of advertisement should be banned, as should consumption in public places. The public should be pointed out the dangers of experimenting with and regularly using drugs. Drugs should be sold only in special stores, with clear indications on dosage, proven and suspected side-effects, and risks of addiction. Each purchase should be registered centrally, to ensure that what's obtained is only used for personal consumption and not for resale. Again, any unauthorized sale should be prosecuted and severely punished.

Cost would have to become another disincentive for drug use. Taxes should raise the cost of drugs to a level just below that at which illegal production and distribution would become lucrative. Moreover, severe penalties would have to be imposed on people who, through their drug use, would endanger or cause harm to others—for example, by driving under the influence. Health and life insurance premiums for drug users should be higher than for non-users, in accordance with the increased risk the drug in question poses to the user's health. On the other hand, any drug user wanting to kick the habit should have access to professional help and treatment, at affordable, income-linked cost.

A crucial question in the debate on drug legalization is what effect legalization would have on the number of users. That's impossible to predict. What is certain is that it does not automatically lead to an increase in consumption. Take the case of Holland, where the use and small scale trade in soft drugs is tolerated: drug use and the number of drug-related deaths is considerably less than in neighboring countries, with much stricter policies.

Not much can be said, then, on the effects of legalization on the number of users. There is clarity, however, on the advantages of legalization and regulation. The first is, as said, the elimination of the unsolicited crime that now accompanies prohibition. Drug related violence between crime groups would disappear, and the influence of organized crime in society would greatly diminish.

A second advantage of legalization would be that it would allow quality control. Limiting the sale of drugs to specialty stores would ensure control on product composition and quality. That would reduce the risk of casualties through overdoses or poisoning, due to the dilution of the pure product with harmful substances. It would also prevent the mixing of soft drugs with hard drugs, a practice sometimes used by dealers to make new addicts.

Regulation would also be financially attractive. The savings in law enforcement would be enormous, whereas taxing the production, distribution and consumption of drugs would generate huge revenues. Among others, this money could be used for the economic and social development of areas with high crime rates, such as the inner cities. Also, it could be used to help fund the rehabilitation of convicts of drug related and other crimes. Thus, unsolicited crime could be brought down even further.

In principle, substituting prohibition with regulation would be a feasible approach for all forms of solicited crime, with advantages similar to those described for drugs. For example, regulation of prostitution could ensure to a greater extent that supply of the service is voluntary rather then forced. Also, it would greatly decrease the possibilities of minors getting involved in the trade. Moreover, it would allow more stringent medical control to protect providers and clients against disease. Especially in poorer countries, this would contribute importantly to public health, notably with regard to the spread of AIDS. Lastly, taxation of the often generous incomes earned with prostitution would yield significant revenues.

Regulation should also be applied to some vices that are now, in spite of their negative side effects, largely unregulated. Most urgent would be to take on the smoking of tobacco. Research on the health hazards of smoking is much more conclusive than that on the risks of drug use—yet cigarettes are freely available in any store. Apart from taxation and the warning that smoking may be dangerous to your health, regulation is, in most countries, virtually absent. Only in the U.S. has a serious beginning been made with protecting non-smokers from the indoor air pollution caused by smokers. Most astonishing is that almost everywhere, children can purchase and smoke tobacco at will. Many become addicted well before coming of age. Also, in few if any countries have measures been taken to protect children, including infants, from cigarette smoke. There are no information campaigns to point out to parents that their smoking habits quadruple the chance that their children contract chronic pulmonary diseases, such as asthma or chronic bronchitis. Advertising is still widely allowed, giving a glamour to smoking to which young people are particularly sensitive. From the point of view of public health, that doesn't make any sense. It would be much more logical to treat tobacco the same way as other drugs. Provision to minors, use in public, and advertisement and promotion should be strictly prohibited. The public should be informed in detail of all proven and suspected health risks. Sales should be made only at special stores, and be centrally registered.

Rehabilitation and treatment

In conclusion, then, the most important step for reducing unsolicited crime is the above suggested regulation of what is now solicited crime. A further reduction could be achieved through a three-way approach. The first component would be correction or rehabilitation, the second, medical treatment, and the third, prevention through forestallment.

As for correction and rehabilitation, we've seen in Chapter IV how judicial systems largely fail in these tasks. Especially imprisonment is ineffective: putting people in jail does not as a rule rehabilitate them. Instead, it deepens and hardens their negative attitudes towards society and, often, sharpens their criminal skills. Moreover, after the sentence is served, it is often difficult for ex-convicts to find employment. Without alternative ways of making a living, offenders are likely to return to crime.

The above calls for an overhaul of prison systems. Reform should make them live up to their official label: correctional facilities. Prisons should focus on rehabilitation, particularly for first-time offenders. Much more so than today, different types of facilities should be created to separate first time and repeat offenders, and to segregate convicts according to the seriousness of their crime.

Rehabilitation should have two components. One should prepare convicts for a successful reentry in economic life. To promote this offenders should, while in prison, be pressed to educate themselves according to their abilities and interests. After serving their prison term, ex-inmates should be helped to find fitting employment. Where necessary, they should be helped to finish educational careers they could not complete in prison.

The second and most important component of rehabilitation would be 'resocialization': instilling, or strengthening, the basic norms and values that regulate social life. The goal, obviously, would be to create or strengthen attitudes that keep a person from doing harm to others and to society as a whole. Specialized staff, such as psychologists and criminologists, should provide counseling by helping people analyze their particular situation and the origins of their behavior. Civics courses should contribute to creating a greater understanding of citizens' rights and obligations in society. Thus, convicts should be made to see clearly the unfairness of victimizing individual persons as a response to perceived injustices in society.

As was briefly mentioned in Chapter IV, recent research has linked various forms of impulsive criminal behavior to biological factors. Adequate medical treatment, combined with the above described social and psychological measures, should help to reduce criminal impulses in the persons involved. Much research still needs to be done: the understanding of the physiological and social causes of criminal and other deviant behavior is still limited. Also, the development of therapy is still in its infancy. Funding research and applying the results should therefore receive a high priority.

Psychological tests, reviews, and interviews should provide insight in the success of resocialization therapy. Passing those tests and reviews should be made a condition for release from prison. Those not showing the needed changes in attitudes should be kept in confinement. Thus, the length of stay in prison would be determined by both the seriousness of the crime and the preparedness to reenter society and lead a normal life.

To make the release from prison dependent on a convict's fitness to reenter society would call for new ways of sentencing. The starting point would be that a mental condition that keeps convicts from recognizing the immorality of their acts is pathological. Because of this pathological condition, repeat of the offense could very well be possible. Further detainment would therefore be in order, both to protect society against that risk and to provide more time for resocialization.

Thus, a sentence would consist of two components. The first, fixed component would have the character of retribution. It would reflect both the seriousness of the crime and the conditions in which it was committed. The second, more open-ended component would be rehabilitation or recovery. If these could be achieved within the period of retribution, release would take place at the moment the latter would be completed. If not, judicial authorities should be able to extend detention, until experts would consider a sufficient degree of rehabilitation has taken place.

Prevention through forestallment

As most law enforcement officials and government campaigns would have it, crime prevention is locking your car, protecting your home with solid locks and an alarm system, and staying out of dangerous neighborhoods. This, however, is more likely to transfer crime than prevent it. A professional crook will not be deterred by a locked car, and refine his methods so he can enter anyway. Or he will look for another car or home, or move to mug an unsuspecting passerby in another part of town. Leaving this form of 'prevention' as an electoral theme for politicians (for whom it is convenient to shift part of the burden of fighting crime to citizens), let's look instead at two other, more promising methods: forestallment and deterrence.

Forestallment is having people refrain from crime for moral reasons. This happens through socialization: the adoption and acceptance of the rules and norms that regulate social life. In the first instance, socialization takes place within the family. Formal education, however, can also contribute importantly. Beginning in day care centers and kindergarten, children can be stimulated in developing norms, values and behavior that facilitate social life and instill respect for other people's rights. In secondary school and thereafter, civics courses such as proposed in Chapter VII and in the above for the rehabilitation of offenders, should become an integral part of curricula. In imaginative ways, these courses should instill in students a clear understanding of their rights as well as their obligations as citizens, in relationship to others and towards society in general.

Another component of forestallment should be to fight the frustration among many of the young males from disadvantaged backgrounds who now make up the bulk of offenders. Frustration can be countered by creating a more promising outlook on life. That should happen through providing opportunities for what psychologists call self-realization: the fulfillment of one's potential as a human being. Non-economic ways of self-realization can be fostered by, for example, engaging in sports or cultural activities. The most important form of self-realization is, however, economic: making a living through work that earns a decent income and is psychologically gratifying.

The key to economic self-realization is an adequate education. As was discussed in Chapter VII, to prepare students in the best possible way for entering the labor market, students should be obliged to remain in school until completing their education. This implies that the principle of compulsory education should be linked not so much to age as to successfully finishing some kind of secondary, job-oriented training.

A good education is not much use if there are no jobs. Although a better education would improve job prospects, today it would still be likely to leave many people without work—especially in depressed areas like the inner cities. To solve this problem, jobs could be created by the programs for sustainable development proposed in previous chapters. Especially the improvement and expansion of economic and social infrastructure and of educational and health care systems would offer huge opportunities for employment. Also, the secondary effects of these activities, including the economic and social revival of inner cities, would be important job creators.

Prevention through deterrence

As was mentioned in Chapter IV, people who commit crimes in an emotional state or out of alienation—like assault in a fit of anger or the mass hysteria of a riot, or the hyped, senseless violence of youth gangs—do not think about the consequences. Therefore, the punishment given for such crimes will not serve as a deterrent. Instead, prevention should aim at forestallment, as indicated above.

With contemplated crime, however, the potential offender does weigh potential benefits against the possible costs: notably, the risk and the consequences of capture. If the risk is high and the consequences are serious, there is a good chance the crime won't take place. Contemplated crime, therefore, can be prevented through deterrence: by increasing the risks of capture and worsening the consequences.

Practically all indirect crime is contemplated. The same goes for most direct crime against property, and much of the unsolicited crime that accompanies solicited crime. With organized and corporate crime, the level of contemplation is even higher. In all these cases, therefore, effective enforcement and severe penalties are effective deterrents. Unfortunately, as we've seen in Chapter IV, the just mentioned crime forms are those for which law enforcement is least effective. Chances of being apprehended are small; in many countries, punishment is mild. This has led to a situation in which, briefly put, crime pays.

To ensure that crime does *not* pay, the law enforcement agencies charged with detection and prosecution will have to be strengthened. Second, laws should be changed and judicial systems overhauled to allow for stricter penalties. Increased chances of getting apprehended for such felonies as tax evasion, illegal dumping of refuse, or giving or receiving bribes would reduce the incentive for engaging in them. Heavy penalties—say, fines of, for example, ten times the potential gains of the crime—would restrain people even further.

Corporate crime is, more than any other form of criminal behavior, contemplated. Therefore forceful law enforcement, including high penalties, can be a highly effective deterrent. To function as such those penalties should be aimed at those responsible: management.

Today, as a rule, the company pays the penalty for breaking the law. Yet fining a company is neither the most fair nor the most adequate means of punishment. It is not fair because those who ultimately pay the bill are not those directly responsible. Fining a company comes down to having shareholders, taxpayers, consumers and workers pay the price. Net profits and therefore, dividends for shareholders, will be less, as will corporate taxes. A raise in product prices may be needed to compensate for the fines. Thus, the bill is passed to consumers. Very high fines can result in bankruptcies. That means employees who most likely had nothing to do with the committed crimes lose their jobs. Meanwhile the actual offenders, that is, the managers who ordered or at least, permitted the violations, go free.

The obvious solution to this problem is to hold managers, notably Chief Executive Officers, personally accountable for offenses committed by the companies they run. Only if they can prove conclusively that lower ranked officials took the initiative for and carried out the illegal actions, without the CEOs knowledge and against company policy, should those lower officials be held responsible.

A form of indirect crime that merits particular attention is corruption in government bureaucracies. Especially in countries where this form of crime is 'socially accepted' it can be countered only by changing attitudes: of officials, clients, the political leadership and the public. Changing attitudes is a long term process. Both government officials and the public must come to see that government institutions can only function well if equal treatment is given to every citizen. Instruction in civics would be a prime instrument for achieving the required changes in attitudes. Moreover, civil servants should receive special training to equip them with both the attitudes and the skills for rendering public service.

Corruption should also be fought through positive incentives. As we saw in Chapter V, a prime cause of petty corruption in poor nations is that officials' wages are so low that corruption is a sheer matter of survival. That is so even for public servants who fulfill key functions, such as police officers. Increasing salaries to levels that would allow a reasonable standard of living would therefore eliminate or at least reduce one of the prime incentives for small scale corruption.

Another way to fight corruption would be to diminish the opportunities to engage in it. One way to do so is by cutting red tape. Where a maze of governmental rules and regulations obstructs the functioning of society, officials are in a perfect position to abuse their authority by demanding payment for their services. Taking away bureaucratic obstacles would therefore both stimulate productive activity and diminish the possibilities for corruption. Also, lesser regulation would mean a lesser need for government personnel. That, in turn, would help the much needed streamlining of state bureaucracies.

Effective law enforcement

In the above we've looked mainly at the possibilities of reducing contemplated crime through rehabilitation and higher penalties. Now, let's consider the complementary approach: more effective law enforcement, so as to increase the chances for offenders getting caught. One strategy would be to enable agencies to perform their task better, by providing them with sufficient funding and adequately training and paying their personnel. That would be especially important for tracing and prosecuting large scale indirect crime. Due to the ever-increasing complexity of communications technology and financial management, fighting such crime requires ever higher levels of expertise and more advanced equipment. Obviously, both carry a cost.

A second way to make law enforcement more effective would be to make it easier to trace the profits of crime. Today, probably the biggest obstacle to prosecuting indirect, organized and corporate crime is formed by the many possibilities to stash illegally obtained funds abroad, in untraceable accounts. The numbered accounts of Swiss banks are the most famous example, but there are many other ways to hide funds from tax collectors and law enforcement agencies. The obvious measure to remedy this situation would be to create a worldwide financial-administrative system. This should register every person or group owning more than a specified amount of capital—say, $20,000.

In many countries, citizens and incorporated groups already have a unique fiscal, social security or other registration number. Simply putting a country code (which could consist of two letters) in front of this number should do the job. All information regarding accounts of over, say, $5,000, should be registered in a central data bank. Upon request the competent national authorities should be given access to these data.

The above proposal would imply the end of numbered or otherwise anonymous bank accounts, and of accounts registered under false names. It would, of course, generate strong resistance. Partly, this would come from capital owners who have tucked away their money in all sorts of tax havens and accounts over which authorities have no control. On the other hand, protests can be expected from countries that up till now have profited from the banking secret. The most famous of these is of course Switzerland, somewhat less well-known is Luxembourg. Not incidentally, these are the two richest countries in the world. No doubt, the chance to get rich of money obtained through crime—notably, the drugs trade, tax evasion and corruption—has helped them to become so. Now, however, it's high time to return all this illegally obtained capital to its original owners. The banking secret should be ended, so that all depositors would be forced to make themselves known. Their data should be fed into the above proposed central register of capital owners; those having obtained their money illegally should be prosecuted. The balance of all accounts for which no claimants would appear should be confiscated. All money thus impounded should be deposited in a special fund, to finance the global programs for sustainable development. That way, at least some of the damages done by its former owners could be compensated for.

You may wonder why doing away with the banking secret and initiating the international registration of wealth have never been proposed. With regard to the latter, banks and governments are likely to argue that it is politically and technically impossible. The technical argument may have made sense twenty and maybe even ten years ago, but not anymore. With current communication and computer technology it should be a readily solvable problem. As for political feasibility, that is a matter of political will. If the governments of major nations would agree, international agreements could be reached fairly easily. You might conclude, then, that those who would have to take the initiative have an interest in not doing so.

Of course, politicians will claim that the countries with a banking secret would be unwilling to cooperate. But countries such as Switzerland and Luxembourg are small and highly dependent on trade with the rest of the world. That means that unified international pressure would be quite effective. True, the proposed measures could have a negative effect on the economies of these nations. That would be too bad, but no argument to maintain a system that makes for unfair competition in banking, and that has already provided these countries with huge riches. There is also no reason to continue condoning banking systems that engage in practices that are prohibited almost everywhere: the trade in stolen goods and the whitewashing of improperly obtained capital.

At the national level also, measures could be taken to trace illegally obtained money. One possibility would be to prohibit the use of cash for any transactions over, say, $2000. Such a measure would force criminals to process any significant sums of illicit money through banks. That would give law enforcement agencies the possibility to trace them and so, obtain leads to other criminal activities.

Fairness

Almost everywhere judicial systems are, to a smaller or larger extent, tilted towards the rich and powerful. This is not limited to the poor being prosecuted and penalized much more harshly than the rich and powerful. Even where equal sentences are meted out these are likely to hit the poor harder than the rich. The most obvious example are fines. The amount of a fine depends on the type and seriousness of the crime. Under the principle of 'equality before the law', the economic position of the offender is not considered. Strictly applied, this principle means that someone with an annual income of $10,000 is fined the same for a particular offense as someone who takes home $100,000 a year—say, $1000. Obviously, such punishment weighs much heavier on the low income offender. That is not only unfair, but also violates the principle of 'equality before the law'.

It would be much more equitable if equality before the law were measured in relative terms, not absolute ones. Penalties for a particular offense should not *be* equal for all, but should be *felt* equally by different offenders. That means that fines should be based on the financial position of the perpetrator—for example, a percentage of his income and wealth. An important additional advantage of this would be that fining would become a more effective deterrent, particularly for the types of indirect crime committed mostly by the rich.

Another element of fairness is the cost of administering justice. Today, it is carried by the taxpayer. Middle and lower class citizens, who make up the large majority of taxpayers, shoulder most of the burden. It would therefore be both logical and fair to have offenders, especially those who in spite of their wealth find it necessary to engage in crime, contribute to these costs to their ability. Such an arrangement would serve as an additional deterrent, especially for wealthy offenders. Moreover, it would generate revenues for making law enforcement and rehabilitation more effective.

Convicted offenders, then, should contribute to the extent possible to the cost of the trial(s), detention and rehabilitation. Moreover, in case of a direct crime, damages should be paid to the victim. In the case of indirect crime, the damage done or money owed (to the state) would be due. Thirdly, the offender would have to pay a penalty in the form of a fine. The amount of this fine should depend both on the seriousness of the offense and on the wealth of the offender. Arrangements could be made in which the total amount due, including the contribution to trial and incarceration costs, would be paid gradually. This could happen through productive labor carried out during detention. If need be, this could be stretched to include payments made after the offender returns to society. Those payments should not, however, be so high or drawn out as to affect reintegration into the community.

Chapter X

IMPROVING GOVERNMENT

The previous chapters lead to the conclusion that the combination of strong, visionary government and a dynamic private sector is the key to development. That's confirmed by recent history: in the past few decades, this blend has created the most striking success stories. The rapid development of East Asian nations such as South Korea, Taiwan and Singapore, and before that Japan, are cases in point. In all these countries forceful government promoted giant economic and, to varying extents, social and political advances. Similarly, the rise of the u.s. to world leadership became possible only through a massive, state-led effort which pulled the nation out of the Great Depression of the 1930s, led it to victory in World War II, and to unprecedented wealth thereafter. In Europe also, visionary political leadership in the decades after World War II led to a period of unparalleled growth. In all these cases, it's been the ability of governments to harness and direct their nations' production capacity that led to impressive development records.

Today, more than ever, strong government is needed to deal with the problems we're facing. To set in motion a process of sustainable development, the productive forces in society have to be mustered and set on the right path. The only institution that can do so is the state. Unfortunately, today the view prevails that the role of government in society, and especially in the economy, should be reduced as much as possible. Development should be left to the 'invisible hand of the market', which will guide us in using our resources in the most efficient way.

The aversion to a strong role of government has several causes. One, discussed in Chapter V, is the preoccupation of people and governments with the economy, which has led to a disproportionate influence of mainstream economic thought on policy making. In economics, the key question is how scarce resources can be used to satisfy demand in the most efficient way. Economic theory holds that such is the case in a perfectly open market. In

economic utopia, therefore, government intervention is reduced to a minimum or eliminated altogether.

A second source of aversion against the state is public opinion. Many
people equate the state to a bunch of bureaucrats whose favorite pastime is to
meddle in people's lives. They consider their tax money is squandered on ill-
conceived projects and oversized bureaucracies, and that because of this
waste, their taxes are too high. They have a point. Yet in practice these flaws
are often less severe than they are made out to be. They are skillfully exploited, however, by self-serving politicians. Playing upon the annoyance of
the public, they manage to instill an even greater dislike of government. And
indignation only increases when politicians who promise change do the same
as their predecessors once they're elected. Thus, politics and government are
increasingly seen as the same thing, and the public's distaste with both has
risen to unprecedented highs.

Although their anger is understandable, people should not let their negative view of politics and government bureaucracies lead them to dismiss the
state. The answer to the problems caused by self-serving politicians and
bureaucrats is not to allow conservative economists and politicians to dis-
member the state and relegate its tasks to the private sector. The better road
is to use past and present experiences, both negative and positive, to make
government more effective, efficient and responsive. For in spite of all past
and present mistakes, a well-functioning, strong state is the core of modern
society. It is the only institution that can guarantee freedom to its citizens,
create the conditions for economic growth, and pave the way for socially
equitable, ecologically sustainable development.

To set us on that path, a radical change is needed in today's singular focus
on short term economic interests. The drive for immediate economic gain must
be replaced by a longer term perspective, based on social justice and responsibility towards future generations. That will require a reversal of the hierarchy
of interests discussed in Chapter v. Politicians must base their decision making
on the medium and long term public interest, not on the short term interests of
constituencies and special interest groups. Problem is, most politicians depend
on the support of these groups to be elected. And as the next election is never
far away, politicians can do little but yield to these short term interests.

A partial solution to this problem would be to give policy makers more
liberty in governing, by reducing the pressure from voters and special interests. One way to do so would be to base electoral systems on proportional instead of district representation. In district representation, a candidate is

chosen by a small, clearly defined part of the electorate: the population of the district. In proportional representation, the candidate is chosen by the entire electorate. That reduces the pressure to give in to specific local or regional interests at the cost of the common good. Even more important, it reduces the disproportionate influence of special interest groups on elections. Today, such groups can focus on districts where their support is instrumental in getting a candidate elected. In proportional representation, that possibility does not exist. Therefore, it allows politicians more leeway to take account of the common good.

Opponents of proportional representation often point to the danger that in elections, no party will gain an absolute majority. Consequently, governments must be formed by a coalition of parties. This, so it is argued, makes for long-winded negotiations and cabinets weakened by differing points of view. In spite of these problems, however, proportional representation has worked quite well in a number of countries, notably in Northern Europe. On the other hand, the political logjam in the U.S. clearly shows the drawbacks of the district system. At the national level, the ties between politicians and their constituencies have made pork-barrel politics the name of the game. The narrow focus on local and regional interests hinders the integrated, focused approach that is needed to solve the nation's problems. As a result, little is done to address growing poverty, crime, the decay of inner cities and the nation's infrastructure, the deterioration of public education, and rising health care costs.

The district system, then, is not adapted to today's policy needs. It is a relic of a past in which representatives of fairly autonomous political units met regularly to discuss matters of common interest, such as coping with an external threat or facilitating international trade. Today, however, many tasks that in the past were taken care of by such small autonomous units have been taken over by national governments. They should therefore be decided upon by nationally elected representatives. Today's district electoral system, in which regionally or locally elected candidates decide on national affairs, is out of date. Especially at a time when society's problems require solutions at the national and international level, politicians who are forced to defend local interests should not be made to decide on issues related to the common good.

More leeway for politicians to govern in the public interest could also be achieved by increasing the intervals between elections. That would give politicians more opportunity for longer-term policy making, and for showing voters the results of their efforts. Also, it would leave them more time to govern. Today some politicians, especially those up for re-election every two years, spend more time campaigning than governing the nation. This is a problem especially in the u.s., with its bi-yearly elections for Congress and four-yearly elections for the presidency. Suppose that intervals between elections would be lengthened to six years, and that all elections (for House, Senate and the Presidency) would take place simultaneously. That would mean representatives and president would have to pander to voters only once every six years instead of two.

In many countries, the biggest obstacle to having elected officials focus on the long term public interest is their dependency on money. As we've seen in Chapter v, money corrupts the democratic process. Financial support obliges a politician to defend the interests of his contributors rather than those of the public at large. Consequently, the interests of wealthy backers are put before the common good.

As discussed in Chapter v, another drawback of a political system that depends on money is that it limits the access of voters to information. Voters' rights are not limited to a secret vote. They also have the right to balanced information on the programs and viewpoints of those competing for their vote. Therefore, all serious parties or candidates should have equal opportunity to present their views. In most North European countries that is already the case: all registered political parties are given the same amount of time to present their views on radio and television. Moreover, expenditure on campaigns is strictly limited, to avoid undue advantages for bigger, better-funded parties.

Public administration

In previous chapters, I pointed to bad government as a prime obstacle to development in the poor countries. I also mentioned that the quality of government depends as much on competent leaders as on a capable and responsive civil service. The problem is that in most poor countries, civil servants do not perceive that their function is to serve the public: instead, they consider their position as a license to serve themselves and their superiors. In the rich nations the idea that civil servants should serve the public has taken more hold. Yet there also, public employees' own needs, the needs of their superiors and those of the organization they work for outweigh the public interest.

Improving government and increasing the responsiveness of civil servants to the needs of the public will require an overhaul of public institutions, particularly in the poor nations. Next to improving technical and management skills, training should aim at changing attitudes. Government employees should come to see themselves as public servants, as employees contracted by taxpayers to provide services as efficiently as possible. That will require quite a change from the present outlook, in which such services are not seen as a right but as a privilege, to be granted to citizens at the discretion of the government employee.

Besides training, the restructuring of public services should aim at a clear definition of the tasks and responsibilities of government institutions. Emphasis should be put on decentralization: the delegation of decision making power from the national to statal, provincial and local levels. Higher levels should provide a policy framework within which lower levels should operate. Within the margins set, civil servants and elected office holders should be given free reign to carry out their tasks as effectively and efficiently as possible.

In many, especially richer countries, with the u.s. as a prime example, decentralization is already quite advanced. In many poor countries, however, decisions that could easily be taken at the local level are taken by faceless bureaucrats in the capital. Long communication channels and lack of knowledge of what's happening at the local level impede effective decision making, and can lead to serious errors. Delegation of decision-making powers can avoid such problems, and increase efficiency, effectiveness and accountability. Efficiency and effectiveness are promoted because local civil servants know the situation in their area, and are in closer contact with the citizens they're supposed to serve. Therefore, they can act more rapidly and adequately then office holders whose offices are hundreds or even thousands of kilometers away. Accountability is fostered because citizens know local civil servants and address them, or the elected officials responsible for them, when there are complaints.

Since the early 1990's, decentralization has become a buzzword in many development institutions, such as the World Bank. What is often insufficiently recognized, though, is that decentralizing decision-making also requires decentralizing budgets. If the delegation of tasks to lower levels is not matched by funding to carry out those tasks, decentralization results in the elimination instead of the reallocation of government tasks. Also, funding should be made available for extra training, so as to put the officials who receive new responsibilities up to the task. In addition to strengthening management and in some cases, technical skills it will be important to change attitudes: instead of waiting for orders, civil servants should come to take action on their own initiative.

Another way to foster efficiency in the dispensing of government services is to privatize them. For successful privatization, several conditions have to be met. First, private enterprise should be able and willing to perform the tasks involved in a more efficient manner than the public sector. Second, there should be no major conflict between the goal of private enterprise, which is to maximize profits, and that of public service: to provide as good a service as possible to all citizens who need it. Third, in the case of essential services dominated by one or two providers—such as drinking water or energy supply—the state should maintain control over decisions on such key items as fees, access and quality.

Reorganization of government agencies would not only imply new attitudes, but also new forms of management and operation. Many recent insights in how to make private companies more effective could also be applied in the public sector, in both rich and poor countries. That could put an end to today's large, rigidly structured hierarchies, with their strongly centralized decision making. Instead, government institutions should be transformed into smaller, more flexible, more autonomous and task-oriented units. Civil servants should get greater leeway in decision making, with initiative being rewarded rather than discouraged by superiors.

To be able to operate effectively such smaller, more flexible units should be given the necessary means and facilities. In particular, they should be able to control their budgets to a much greater extent than is now the case. Also, reward systems should be created that would award performance and results rather than strict adherence to rules and procedures.

New attitudes, training and new forms of management would not by themselves be sufficient to achieve effective government. At least as important would be incentives for change, both positive and negative. On the positive side, civil servants should come to earn as well as their counterparts in the private sector. At the very least, salaries should be raised to such an extent that corruption would no longer be needed to attain a decent standard of living. Especially in the judiciary and the police, payment should reflect the key importance of these branches for the protection of citizen's rights and effective government.

Conversely, civil servants, especially those in law enforcement and other positions of authority, should be punished severely for any abuses of power, self-enrichment or other infractions. Effective monitoring and control systems should be installed, to which members of the public who would feel they had been wronged should have easy access. In other words, at all levels of government accountability to the public, through effective control and rapid action in the case of transgressions, should ensure to the extent possible that civil servants carry out their duties in an efficient and just manner.

Making peace

In the previous chapters, it's become clear that for sustainable development, close international cooperation is required. Such cooperation is crucial to address all problems that reach across national borders: the environment, the economy, crime, poverty, and war. An essential step towards this cooperation would be to increase the role of international organizations, particularly the United Nations.

A greater role for the U.N. is especially important in the case of armed conflict. Since the demise of the former East Bloc, the U.N. role in conflict management has already increased considerably. Nevertheless, intervention as a peace keeper still depends on all parties involved accepting that role. Usually, that is the case only when those parties realize there is little to gain from continuing the war. The U.N. is powerless to act, however, as long as one party still sees advantages in carrying on the fighting. The problem is that the U.N. has no mandate for peace *making*: the use of force to prevent the warring parties from annihilating each other and, most importantly, from harming civilians.

There are two main impediments to peace enforcement. One is that the U.N. does not have its own troops: U.N. forces are troops on loan from member nations. That puts strict limits on their deployment. Especially politicians from rich nations have to minimize the risk of casualties, out of fear of a political backlash at home. This risk avoidance makes U.N. troops hostage to the more aggressive forces in the conflict: threats against peace keepers are often sufficient to impede more forceful intervention.

The second factor inhibiting peace making is that U.N. mandates refer to nation states, not peoples. Consequently, intervention in internal conflicts, such as civil wars, is very difficult, and action is almost impossible when a democratically elected government is deposed. Unfortunately, almost all recent armed conflicts are civil wars, a trend that's likely to continue in the future. Under its current mandate, in almost all these cases the U.N. is forced to stay on the sidelines. In the meantime, civilians fall victim to the warring factions, and to the economic and social disruption caused by the fighting.

The solution to these problems is twofold. First, the mandate of the U.N. should be aimed not so much at protecting the sovereignty and integrity of nation states as at protecting the sovereignty and integrity of people. The second is to provide the U.N. with the means to carry out its mandate: its own armed forces.

The idea would not be to have U.N. forces rush headlong into large scale military operations whenever a conflict occurs. Rather, it would be to strengthen U.N. diplomatic powers. In most cases, the threat of armed intervention would be sufficient to reach a political solution. Mediation would become much more effective, and would evolve into arbitration. Armed intervention would be strictly a matter of last resort, to fall back on when diplomacy would fail altogether.

A standing U.N. army should be highly mobile, consisting of well-equipped ground forces with adequate air transport and air-ground support. For further naval and air support it should be possible to call on the major powers which, undoubtedly, would maintain at least part of their own armed forces. Other, smaller nations, however, could eliminate or greatly reduce their military, as their functions would be taken over by the U.N. forces.

Maintaining well paid, equipped and trained U.N. forces would require a substantial contribution from member states. However, these costs could be financed easily from the savings obtained by the partial or complete abolition of national armed forces. Countries who'd do so could also provide materiel and personnel. Incorporation in U.N. forces should, however, be made dependent on thorough screening. Selection criteria should include not only military training and skills, but also understanding of and adherence to human rights and in general, wholehearted support for the principles of the U.N.

As said, the regional presence of a permanent U.N. military force would provide the opportunity for many smaller nations to abolish their army. Of course, total disarmament would surely run into major opposition from die-hard nationalists and the military itself. But most countries can do perfectly well without armed forces. The example has already been set by a small Central-American country, Costa Rica, which in 1948 decided to abolish its army. At least partly because of that decision, it has since turned into what is by far the wealthiest and most developed country in Central America. Interestingly, it has never faced a serious military threat. Yet it is bordered in the

South by Panama and in the North by Nicaragua, both countries that over the last twenty years have been politically unstable, with the military playing a central role. Most notably, Costa Rica had the courage to disarm unilaterally, without the security of a U.N. force able and willing to protect its sovereignty. In contrast, the arrangement proposed above would provide, first, the guarantee that the U.N. would counter any act of aggression. Secondly, the chances of such aggression would be minimized as, under the proposed arrangement, neighboring countries would also disarm.

Avoiding war

Disarmament and a growing role for U.N. forces in international and national disputes would greatly contribute to world peace. However, these measures would not control the causes of war. The only effective way to avoid war is to minimize the chance that the call to arms gets popular support.

Especially in non-democratic nations, ruthless leaders use propaganda and misinformation to whip up nationalist aggression. If skillfully managed, this can evolve in a popular demand to go to war. In a democracy, with more room for dissenting voices and freedom of information, such indoctrination of the public is more difficult. Still, at times politicians in democratic states are also able to generate popular support for a war, even an aggressive one. That's the case especially if they receive the support of an uncritical, nationalistic press. On the other hand, a genuinely free, pluralist press, guided by the ideal of unbiased reporting, is a crucial instrument for peace. In a society where elected officials are followed critically and where all differing viewpoints are heard, generating the mass hysteria required to support state violence will be close to impossible.

Most important in the prevention of war is instilling in people a critical, rational frame of mind that will lead them to oppose any form of warmongering. The key to that is education. Citizens should be brought up with a critical attitude towards their leaders, and tolerance towards people from other faiths, nationalities, and ethnic origins. They should develop an aversion to dogmatism, extremism, and authoritarianism. Leaders who advocate violence and war can be opposed effectively only if a majority of the population holds a deep-seated respect for human rights. Most importantly, people should acquire the reasoning capacity and empathy that will keep them from blaming a whole group for the acts of a few of its members.

After all, it is this tendency to assign collective blame that leads to the victimization of unarmed citizens, including women, children and elderly people.

A new approach to politics

How much can today's politicians contribute to generating the above proposed changes? As things stand, not very much. The basic problem is, as we've seen in Chapter v, that politics is practiced according to outdated principles. Its approach of conflictive engagement was useful in the past, when it served the purposes of rulers competing for power and wealth. Today politicians, like the rulers of old, still have conflicting interests. But the people whose interests they claim to represent do not. People are served by peace and cooperation, not conflict. Today more than ever, the archaic approach to politics is an obstacle to the cooperation that is needed to address the world's problems and further the common good.

The need, then, is for a new brand of politics, based on cooperation, reason and fairness. Such cooperation should bring to an end the arduous negotiations and talks that drag on for years or even decades, at a cost of millions of taxpayer dollars, without yielding satisfactory results. Instead, it should lead to rapid, workable and equitable solutions for global or regional problems— from the rational use of the world's natural resources to socially equitable economic development, and from fighting crime to fostering peace between and within countries.

The new politics should be based on 'constructive' rather than conflictive engagement. Politicians should no longer try to bargain their way to a maximum result at the cost of the other party. Instead, they should aim for an equitable solution, to be arrived at through the rapid settlement of differences. Where in spite of such an approach an agreement could not be reached, the parties involved should submit to arbitration. That is, the dissenting parties should accept, unconditionally, the judgment of a third, independent and impartial referee.

In some cases, such arbitrators could be informally agreed upon by the two contending parties. In others, and always as a least resort, the parties should be obliged to present their case to an international court—such as today's International Court of Justice of the u.n., established in The Hague in The Netherlands. When needed, that is, when one—or both—parties would refuse to carry out the decision of the court, that decision should be enforced by the U.N. forces.

The principle of arbitration is a logical consequence of the need to have society function effectively. Without arbitration, the contending parties may go on bickering for years, without coming to an agreement. Such conflict hinders and, when occurring on a large scale, endangers the functioning of any group, organization or institution. Therefore, even the most primitive societies have created mechanisms for arbitration, to which judgement the quarrelling parties are obliged to submit. In modern society this mechanism is civil litigation, with the judge functioning as the impartial authority by whose ruling the contending parties must abide.

Nowhere is arbitration needed more than at the international level. Yet nowhere is it more absent. The main problem is that politicians acting from a position of power don't want to submit to international arbitration. In a setting of conflictive engagement, they have no incentive to do so. By using their power they can achieve an outcome that, although far from equitable, is beneficial for their country—at least in the short term. This explains why the U.S., the most powerful country in the world and therefore the biggest beneficiary of conflictive engagement, is so averse to submitting to the judgement of international institutions. Also, it explains at least partially why politicians, particularly those from powerful nations, claim that submitting to arbitration is contrary to the national interest. In some specific cases, it may—just as the verdict in a civil court of law may go against the more powerful party. Yet in the longer run, everyone is better off when in all disputes an equitable solution is reached and carried out. Few people will dispute that at national, state or local level, administering justice according to the rule of law is to be preferred over the most powerful party getting its way—simply because it is more powerful. Yet at the international level, the right of the strongest continues to prevail.

Still, many politicians, especially those from powerful nations such as the U.S., will continue to attack the idea of submitting to arbitration. They will also label naive the idea of harmoniously solving international political problems through constructive engagement, reason and fairness. They will claim that the trust required for such an approach is totally lacking in the international arena. To a certain extent they are right. Yet, as we've seen in the above, the reason for that lack is not that conflict is the natural condition of international relations. It is that politicians generate and feed conflictive engagement for their own good. The challenge, therefore, is not only to create a new kind of politics, based on genuine cooperation, but to create new attitudes. Within the current political context that is unlikely to happen. Attitudes are hard to change, and the personal interest of politicians to keep politics in the sphere of conflictive engagement is too great. Instead, a complete restructuring of the political landscape will be needed. In Chapter XIII, some suggestions will be made for a strategy to achieve just that.

Part 3

MONEY

'All truth passes through three stages. First, it is ridiculed. Second, it is violently opposed. Third, it is accepted as self-evident.'

Arthur Schopenhauer, German philosopher

Chapter XI

COSTS, BENEFITS, AND FINANCING

Sustainable development is going to cost: carrying out the measures proposed in this book would come to trillions of dollars. The most expensive components by far would be the development of economic, social and water management infrastructure, and the conversion from nonrenewable to renewable energy. However, as implementation would take several decades, the cost would be distributed accordingly. Meanwhile, the corresponding investments would generate strong economic growth, which would help raise the revenues for further investment. Even so, generating trillions of dollars for investment in sustainable development is inconceivable in today's economic, financial and political setting.

A 'basic' program for sustainable development, however, could be carried out at only a fraction of the cost of the overall plan. This program should aim to eradicate destitute poverty and to address the most urgent environmental problems. The first goal should be achieved by providing the poor with access to adequate health care, education, and ways to make a living—by employment in land and water conservation programs, allotment of agricultural land, and financing small scale enterprises. The second aim would call for the protection of natural ecosystems, increasing energy efficiency, and checking the most serious forms of pollution and soil degradation.

One such basic program is described in Agenda 21, the background document for the United Nations Conference on the Environment and Development (UNCED), held in Rio de Janeiro in June 1992. It contains proposals for pollution control, the sustainable exploitation of nonrenewable raw materials, the preservation of ecosystems, population control, and the alleviation of destitute poverty. Among others, it proposes aid to the developing countries for limiting air pollution caused by burning coal, and for constructing and fixing sewer systems, cleaning up toxic dumps, and reforestation. The officials involved in drawing up the plan estimate its total cost at $125 billion a year.

Agenda 21 leaves us to deal with environmental degradation in the rich countries and the former East Bloc. Cost estimates for a program for pollution control in the rich countries vary between 250 and 350 billion dollars over a 20 year period. For Eastern Europe, the World Bank estimates that a similar amount is needed. A high estimation would put the total cost for the two regions at $800 billion over 20 years, or $40 billion a year. Add this to the $125 billion of Agenda 21, and include another $35 billion per year for providing the destitute poor with basic education and health care, employment, land, and investment capital. That would put the total cost for a basic sustainable development program at $200 billion per year.

Although that may seem a lot of money, it's not that much when we look at the size of the world economy. In 1992, it would have been approximately 1% of the world's GNP. Financing would have been possible with an oil tax of $8 per barrel of crude—about $0.19 per gallon. Alternatively, reducing tax evasion to one third of its present levels could yield a comparable amount.

The point is that the most urgently required measures are costly, but by no means unaffordable. It is a simple matter of priorities. Moreover, payment should be seen as an investment that will earn itself back. The demand resulting from hundreds of millions of people escaping destitute poverty will provide a huge boost to the global economy. Labor productivity will increase because of better health and schooling. The economic cost of pollution will be reduced: purifying drinking water will become cheaper, and damage from air pollution to buildings, forests and crops will decrease. Other benefits include a rise in agricultural production, due to the greater availability of water and the control of erosion and salinization. Also, the life of reservoirs will be prolonged, hydro energy generation increased, and flooding and the clogging of waterways diminished.

To get an idea of the returns on investment in environmental protection, consider the following figures. For Mexico, the economic losses caused by pollution, the destruction of ecosystems and the wastage of natural resources have been estimated at some 15% of the country's GNP. For Germany, one of the most environmentally minded countries in the world, an annual cost of 4% of GNP has been calculated.[1] Assuming most countries will be in this range, let's estimate the global cost of environmental degradation, conservatively, at 5% of the world's gross annual product. That's about $1 trillion yearly. Let's suppose, again very conservatively, that the above-mentioned programs would prevent half the estimated damages: $500 billion. At a cost of $200 billion a year, that's a 250% return. And that's not counting the positive medium and long term effects on human health and productivity, nor the prevention or reduction of the effects of regional and global climate change.

It is therefore not only necessary, but also economically feasible to finance programs such as Agenda 21. So why doesn't it happen? The answer to this question was already given in the preceding chapters: mainstream economic thought, the short term interests of leaders, their lack of vision, and the consequent lack of leadership.

Mainstream economic thought holds that the only way to allocate resources efficiently is through the market, that is, through the unhindered interplay between producers and consumers. If private enterprise is given the means and freedom to go about its business, the invisible hand of the market will allocate society's resources in the best possible way. Yet the above proposed measures would have to be financed by extracting or at best, withholding money from the private sector, and channeling it to the government. According to economic theory, such funds would be spent less efficiently than by the private sector. Therefore, there would be less economic growth. Moreover, the taxes needed to finance the measures would raise prices and reduce expendable income. This would further reduce growth, as well as cost jobs and cut into profits and investment.

Politicians' short-term interests surface in the wooing of voters with tax cuts and smaller government. That sells well after decades of running up debts, misspending tax money, and presenting the bill to taxpayers when things go wrong. It sounds attractive to lower and middle income groups that since the early 1980s have seen their incomes stagnate. And it sits even better with the rich who, so far, have been by far the greatest beneficiaries of tax cuts.

Lack of vision translates into the slavish following of what was already discussed above: mainstream economic thought. Thus, politicians ape economists in stating that society's problems will be solved if market forces are given free reign, and government and taxes are cut. Economic growth will allow everyone to get rich or at the very least, make a decent living. Market forces will see to it environmental protection, education, health care, and the expansion of our economic and social infrastructure take place in the most efficient way. Implicitly, it is also assumed that the market will see to it that future generations will have the energy, raw materials and ecological resources they need to maintain a decent standard of living. The only task for politicians is to create the conditions for market forces to do their wholesome work.

The lack of leadership shows most clearly when politicians hide behind public opinion when faced with tough decisions. Thus, they claim that there is not enough popular support for investment in the environment and the fight against poverty. They may be right. That, however, is where leadership comes in: popular support must be generated by convincing people of the need for change. The basic spirit is there. That is shown by the fact that many citizens are prepared, time and again, to contribute to help people who've been hit by disaster, either at home or abroad. However, rather than kindling this spirit to gain support for investment in sustainable development, the political establishment takes the safer way of pandering to voters' short term concerns.

The political leadership of the poor countries does even worse. The excuse that their countries' debts leave little room for spending on education, health care and natural resource management goes only so far. Although the pressure on budgets is huge, most governments could allocate the remaining funds much better. Less spending on the military, on bloated government bureaucracies and on prestigious projects would be a good start. Simultaneously, effective taxation could greatly increase state revenues. That this does not happen is much more a political and particularly a moral problem than an economic or financial one. The top layers of society simply refuse to contribute even a minor proportion of their riches to alleviate the distress of their fellow citizens.

Obviously, then, a change in attitude of those who govern, and of those who elect them, is needed. The rich must be forced to give up some of their perks, and return to society some of the wealth they have amassed over the last decades. At the same time, government should clean up its act: stop squandering public resources, and reorient spending to where it is really needed.

Cutting spending

One effective way to save on government spending is to reduce the size of state bureaucracies. In many, especially poor countries state payrolls have grown far beyond what is needed to fulfill effectively the core tasks of government. Even in the rich nations where—relatively speaking—the state functions best, its institutions have often grown out of proportion. What's worse, many have developed into bureaucracies whose primary purpose is to serve its own members, not the citizenry.

Another already mentioned possibility for major cutbacks is defense. The reduction of standing armies to smaller, leaner forces would result in large scale reductions in military spending. So would increased control over military expenditure and defense contractors, and better procurement procedures. The largest savings could be obtained through the abolition of national armies in exchange for U.N. security forces, as proposed in Chapter X. The contribution to such forces would only be a fraction of the cost of maintaining a national army.

Better government budgeting would be another way of saving funds. Today, budgets are determined less by needs and priorities than by tradition, lobbying and power. Each ministry, department, institution and agency competes for funding, trying to get as large a slice of the pie as possible. Once budgets are allocated, the most important task is to spend it all. The worst that can happen to an agency is to *not* spend the money allotted to it. That will lead, in the next round of allocations, to a budget reduction, with the argument that apparently more funding was asked for than was needed. Most likely, the funds saved will go to a department that came up short. In other words, spending efficiency is punished by budget reductions, while spendthrifts are rewarded with a budget increase or (in periods of spending cuts) with smaller reductions.

To rationalize government spending a different approach to budgeting is needed. There should be more flexibility in budget allocation, so that expenditure can be adjusted to needs and priorities. Spending efficiency should be rewarded by increasing the possibilities for the agencies and departments involved to finance new, promising programs and projects. On the other hand, inefficient government institutions, providing little bang for the buck, should be held accountable. Budgets should be cut and, much more so than today, personnel should be replaced by more capable management and staff.

Fewer tax breaks

Tax avoidance—the legal use of loopholes in tax laws to reduce one's tax bill—is a very effective means for wealthy people to increase their net income. The potential to do so is clear from the fact that in all countries with a functioning tax system, 'financial consulting' is a lively and highly profitable industry. The thousands of dollars that advisors, consultants and brokers charge for their services are, of course, only affordable for the wealthy. The savings are such, however, that the cost of good advice earns itself back rapidly.

In addition to abolishing tax shelters, subsidies, either direct or in the form of tax deductions, should be cut. Particular attention should be paid to those measures that primarily benefit the rich. One example was already mentioned in Chapter VIII: agricultural subsidies, of which some 80% ends up with wealthy farmers, agro-industries and traders. Another is the deduction of costs for doing business, many of which are little more than fringe benefits for high level employees. Executives annually receive tens of thousands of dollars in kind, in the form of lunches, dinners and other forms of entertainment in fancy restaurants, hotels, nightclubs, country clubs and resorts. The amounts of money involved are stunning. For example, in 1991 the Japanese tax service reported that the private sector had reported as tax deductible business costs the equivalent of $76 billion. This money was spent on business lunches, dinners, golf outings and other forms of diversion. One might expect a comparable amount in the U.S.; in Europe, with a more frugal corporate culture, it might be less. A conservative estimate of some $150 billion worldwide might not be far beside the mark. And that's not even counting the free fare our diplomats and politicians are enjoying.

Another subsidy that would merit pruning is tax deductions on mortgage payments. Some subsidy for homeowners is justifiable—although a system such as the home voucher program proposed in Chapter VII would be preferable. Present systems, however, are disproportionately tilted towards the rich. Let's compare. Someone with a $500,000 mortgage (and the house and income to match it) can, with a 30% income tax rate and annual interest payments of 10%, deduct $1500 a year (30% of the $50,000 to be paid in interest). For someone with a $50,000 mortgage, this amount would be only $1.500.

In countries with a progressive tax rate, the advantage for the $500,000 mortgage is even greater. Suppose there are two rates, 50% for the higher bracket, and 30% for the lower. As the wealthy home owner will be in the 50% bracket, his tax deduction will come to $25,000. The deduction of the owner with a $50,000 mortgage, in the 30% income tax bracket, remains at $1.500. Obviously, people who do not have a mortgage, because they cannot afford to own their own house, get no deduction at all.

As long as a fairer system, such as the home voucher system proposed in Chapter VII, is not in the works, home owners should be given the opportunity to deduct mortgage payments from their taxes. However, these deductions should be capped, that is, be limited to a predetermined amount that reflects the value of standard housing. If people want to live in larger, more luxurious and therefore more expensive houses, fine. That's their choice. But the state and therefore the taxpayer should not have to contribute to their more lavish lifestyle.

In addition to tax avoidance and unequitable subsidies, tax evasion and corruption should also be tackled. In Chapter IV we've seen how as a result of these forms of indirect crime, the world's treasuries have to forego hundreds of billions of dollars each year. Effective law enforcement, supported by the genuine political will to address money laundering (the bringing of illegally obtained money into the legal financial circuit), hidden money transactions and numbered bank accounts, would greatly increase tax revenues. At world level, reducing tax evasion by a factor two or three could render hundreds of billions of dollars a year; confiscation of illegally obtained capital could yield even more.

Taxes on the rich

Raising revenue for investment in sustainable development will also involve increased taxation. Today, that's a no-no. Worldwide, economists and politicians say taxes have to be lowered. Voters agree, and solidly trash politicians who want to raise them. That's because they think higher taxes will mean less disposable income. That, however, depends on which taxes will be raised, and for whom.

For sustainable development, it is necessary to raise taxes on the rich. That's little more than fair. After all, as we've seen in Chapter I, the rich have fared extremely well since the early 1980s—at the cost of the rest of the population. I already mentioned, in Chapter I, that from 1981 to 1990, the bottom 70% of U.S. income earners lost 20% in real income, whereas the top 30% gained 9%.[2] The biggest winners were the very rich: in the U.S., the richest 1% of the population confiscated 70% of the economic growth of the decade.[3] In 1990, with an average annual income of $617,000, this group received 13.5% of all income before taxes, and 12.8% of all after-tax income.[4]

The highest income groups, especially top managers, have benefitted not only from income tax cuts but also from raises in salaries, bonuses and other perks and benefits. Their incomes have risen much faster than those of lesser paid workers: in 1977 top managers earned 44 times the average wage, in 1997, 209 times.[5] Overall, this means that an ever larger share of the national income goes to the rich. U.S. Census Bureau figures show that in 1994, the richest 5% of U.S. households earned 21.2% of the national income—up from 16.6% in 1969. Together with the next 15%, they were good for almost half the national income: 49.1%, up from 43.0% in 1969. Over the same period, the poorest 20% of households saw their share of the national income decline from 4.2% to 3.6%.[6]

High time, then, to take back some of the windfalls of the rich, in order to finance activities for the common good. The most obvious way to do so would be to make income taxes more progressive: to let higher incomes pay a higher percentage of their income in taxes. For the U.S., let's look at a measure that would affect only households earning over $75,000 a year— roughly, the richest 20%. Together, this group is good for a total annual income of about $1.47 trillion. Increasing the percentage of their income paid in taxes by 10 (from the current, roughly estimated, 40% to 50%) would yield an extra $147 billion a year. Hitting those earning over $150.000 a year—roughly equivalent to the richest 5% of households—with an additional 10% would yield an additional $63 billion. Thus, in the U.S. alone a moderate raise in taxes, aimed exclusively at the richest 20% of the population, could yield well over $200 billion a year.[7]

National budgets of poor nations would also benefit greatly from higher taxes on the rich. Although rich households are not nearly as numerous as in the U.S., they often own larger shares of their countries' wealth. Yet as we've seen in previous chapters, they pay few or no taxes: tax rates are usually low, and evasion is the rule rather than the exception. In many poor countries, therefore, effectively applied progressive income and property taxes could multiply government revenues.

The worldwide raising of income taxes on the richest 20% of households in each nation, then, could easily generate an extra $400 to $500 billion in tax revenues each year. That would be enough to pay for a basic program for sustainable development; moreover, it would leave money to spare for, for example, reducing or eliminating budget deficits, and improving public services such as health care and education.

The lower and middle income groups, who make up the overwhelming majority of voters, would have nothing to loose and much to gain from a tax raise on the rich. Making that clear shouldn't be too hard. Neither should it be difficult to convince them that to raise taxes on the highest incomes would be little more than fair, considering the enormous wealth the rich have been extracting from the rest of society since the 1980s, and continue to extract today.

The lower and middle incomes, then, should come to realize that they've been had, and that the scam continues until today. Moreover, they should grasp that this scam takes on ever more grotesque proportions. The most recent example is the proposal to have everyone pay the same percentage of his/her income in taxes—the so-called flat tax—raised in the U.S. 1996 election campaign. Those efforts should be exposed for what they are: self-serving schemes by the privileged to appropriate an even greater share of society's wealth than they already have.

Of course, conservative economists, politicians and other representatives of vested interests manage to come up with a host of reasons why taxes on the rich should be lowered rather than raised. The first is that riches to the rich will create economic growth: an argument based on the myth that the rich will invest their newly earned money in productive activities. We've already seen in Chapter 1 that this assumption is largely wrong: the enormous growth of the international financial circuit is proof that most of the money is used for speculation. Yes, there are those who invest additional wealth in production, as there are those who spend it on still more luxurious consumption. But there is no reason to assume that with regard to productive investment, the rich do a better job than their less well-off fellow citizens or, for that matter, the government. What's worse, when speculation ends in a crash, lower and middle income taxpayers are left with the short end of the stick.

Another well-worn argument for low tax rates for the rich is that high rates take away the incentive for entrepreneurship. If the rich don't get enough compensation, so the argument goes, they won't work as hard and take as many risks. That's nonsense. Although entrepreneurs may claim to be in business for the money, that's not their main driving force. Psychological fulfillment is. Entrepreneurs will continue to do business even if a large part of their income goes to taxes. That's obvious from the fact that the most successful entrepreneurs have made much more money than they will ever be able to spend. Yet most of them keep on working 70 hours a week or more well beyond retirement age.

A look at the Northern European countries is also illustrative. There, upper bracket income tax rates have been lowered from highs of 80% in the 1970s, to about 60% in the 1990s. Still, these nations were, and are, among the wealthiest in the world, with a thriving entrepreneurial climate.

Apparently, power, status, and the thrills of entrepreneurship and risk-taking are what drives business people. Sure, they'll grumble about higher taxes. They've done so in the past, and will do so in the future. But raising or lowering taxes is not going to make a difference: these people will be just as productive as before.

Another argument against high taxes for the rich is 'unfairness'. The rich, so it is claimed, work hard for their money, and earn a lot because they have special skills and talents that are relatively scarce. By applying these faculties, they contribute more to society than others. That's why their reward is just, and why it's not fair that the state takes away a large share of their income through taxation.

More nonsense. True, there are those who have high incomes and work very hard for them. But there are also many rich people who work very little, or not at all. Whereas on the other end of the economic scale, there are millions who work hard and make peanuts. Often, they have jobs that are so tedious, monotonous, unpleasant and sometimes, unhealthy, that even aside from the low pay, people with high incomes would never trade places with them. 'But ...', economists will argue, '... these people lack special skills and therefore don't contribute as much to society as their higher paid colleagues!' Yet wages do not necessarily reflect usefulness to society. Who does more useful work, a construction worker making $20,000 a year building homes, schools and hospitals, or an investment banker or litigation lawyer making millions which, either directly or indirectly, are paid by taxpayers and consumers?

Salaries and other forms of income, then, do not necessarily reflect the contribution people make to society. Often, they do not even adequately indicate the contribution to the organization that pays them. In a free society, there is little that can be done against that. But something can be done about a situation in which a small clique confiscates a disproportionate and growing share of society's wealth. This imbalance should be redressed by redirecting enough of the flow of riches to guarantee, to the extent possible, that the basic needs of all people, now and in the future, are met.

Higher taxes on high incomes, then, should be seen as a means to an end: the common good. Lower and middle income groups can, because of their limited incomes, contribute only moderately to generating the investment capital needed for sustainable development. It is logical, and reasonable, that the rich are obliged to pay the rest of the bill.

Other taxes

In Chapter VIII, environmental taxes were discussed as a way to promote sustainable behavior and raise money for investment in sustainable development. Problem is, an environmental tax is an indirect tax, that is, a tax paid through a surcharge on the price of goods and services. Indirect taxes do not distinguish between buyers: rich or poor, everyone has to pay the same. This means that indirect taxes affect lower incomes more than higher ones, because the price rise caused by the surcharge will cost them a greater share of their income. As the lower income groups in both rich and poor countries have been hit hard enough over the last decade, indirect taxes on commonly used goods and services should be avoided as much as possible.

Still, environmental taxes are unavoidable. Taxing the unsustainable use of resources is an essential incentive for changing to more sustainable behavior. Moreover, environmental taxes would be great revenue raisers: worldwide, each dollar added to an oil tax levied per barrel of crude would raise an extra $25 billion. Therefore, rather than forego environmental taxes to protect lower and middle incomes, the latter should be compensated. One option would be to raise the amount of income over which no income tax is due, or lower the rate of the first tax bracket. Education and health care fees could be reduced, as could obligatory payments for social security. Also, proceeds from environmental taxes should be used for stimulating energy alternatives. For example, the higher cost of heating and transport resulting from an oil tax could be offset by subsidies for solar heating, home insulation, electrically powered vehicles and mass transit.

In addition to compensation by the state, consumers could also seek to offset price rises due to environmental taxes by buying selectively. Today, many products are much more expensive than warranted by the cost of production and distribution. Advertising can increase the price of consumer products by as much as 50%. Consumers should be made aware of the fact that as a result, they pay far more for many goods and services than is necessary. Here, there would be a key role for consumer organizations. As they already do today, they should test products, compare prices and point out the best buys to the public. Making such information easily accessible to consumers, especially to those belonging to lower income groups, would be crucial in helping them increase their purchasing power.

Apart from environmental taxes there are various other possibilities for levying indirect taxes, with a much lesser impact on lower and middle income groups. One would be a tax on luxury goods that normally are bought only by the rich. Take cars: surcharges could be levied on large, luxurious vehicles. Such taxation would not affect lower income buyers who buy smaller models. Since size and luxury are directly related to engine size and fuel use, such a tax would have the additional advantage of stimulating the use of more 'environment friendly' cars. Similarly, 'luxury taxes' could be levied on second and third homes, private planes and yachts, and on other goods and services for the upper class.

Indirect taxes should also be levied on products that are health risks. Thus, taxes on tobacco and (hard) liquor could be raised, especially in countries where they are still low. The same would go for cigarettes. If the use of drugs were regulated as proposed in Chapter IX, there would be enormous potential for taxation. Considering the amounts of money involved in the drug trade today, the yield could well amount to tens of billions of dollars per year.

Another indirect tax with great potential would be the one on security and currency transactions proposed in Chapter VI. Nobel-laureate James Tobin has suggested a 0.5% tax on foreign exchange transactions. At today's volume of transactions, that's been estimated to raise more than $1.5 trillion a year.[8] It would be likely, however, that a Tobin tax would result in a significant decrease in the number of transactions, and therefore, lower proceeds. Still, it would be a major revenue raiser, especially if it were also levied on the trade in securities. As indicated in Chapter VI, the resulting increase in the cost of speculation would have the additional advantage of bringing more stability to financial markets.

Chapter XII

MONEY CREATION

The need for money creation

The measures proposed in the previous chapter would raise enough money to pay for a basic program for sustainable development, aimed at the conservation of natural resources, pollution control, and the elimination of destitute poverty. They would also allow a start on the conversion to renewable energy, the improvement of education, and the strengthening of government services. It would not, however, be sufficient to cover the cost of a global effort to reclaim agricultural land lost due to erosion and silting. Nor would it allow the building of a global infrastructure for water catchment and management, or cover the cost of providing all people with acceptable housing. More money would also be needed for developing the world's economic infrastructure (transport, communications and energy generation), for child development guidance starting in the first few months of life and, in poor countries, the pension and child support funds proposed in Chapter VII. For a complete sustainable development program, then, more money would be needed than could be raised by the measures proposed in Chapter XI.

So where to get it? More government lending would be unwise: budget deficits and national debts are already at record highs. Worse, in the coming decades spending by the governments of the rich nations is likely to increase even without investment for sustainable development, as graying populations will make growing demands on health care budgets and social security. In the current context, therefore, the possibilities for large scale public investment in sustainable development are minimal. So what's to be done?

The answer is to create money, to be used by governments for investment in sustainable development. Money creation for the state is, of course, the exact opposite of what economists, politicians, and other experts consider as sound monetary and economic policy. Indeed, it's one of the worst sins against economic dogma: the epitome of financial, economic and political irresponsibility. An explanation is therefore in order. First, we'll take a closer look at what money really is, and second, we'll determine what it has become under the influence of mainstream economic thought.

Money and faith

Money was invented to facilitate trade. Using money—be it in the form of coins, bills, shells or other easily handled objects—for the purchase and sale of commodities meant a great advance over the bartering of goods. With barter, a party wanting to trade commodity one for commodity two has to find another party, interested in obtaining commodity one and in possession of and willing to trade commodity two. The use of money, however, makes it possible to sell commodity one to any interested party—independent of whether that party has commodity two, or not. With the proceeds, commodity two can be purchased from any party willing to sell it. Thus, money allows for a much more flexible process of exchange. The idea is so practical that it is used in all but the simplest of societies, with few members and little to exchange.

What money really does, then, is to allow the separation of the two components of exchange: sale and purchase. That has an important additional advantage: it facilitates hoarding, or saving. Money takes up very little space and does not spoil, as many commodities, especially agricultural ones, do. Hoarding also allows for accumulation, and the trade in money. Those needing money—to purchase a commodity or to invest in producing one—can borrow it from those who have accumulated it. Later, the borrowed amount is returned with interest: a premium that makes it attractive for owners to lend their money rather than keep it to themselves.

Money, then, is a symbol depicting a certain value. It is used to facilitate two of the most basic economic activities: trade and accumulation. Its use depends on a general agreement to accept it as an instrument for payment. That was the case in the past, and continues to be so today, in modern society. The acceptance of money is based on the faith that others will accept the coins or bills at some point in the future, in exchange for a good or service. Moreover, to serve its purpose, users of money should be confident that money will retain its value. That is, it should be possible to exchange it for commodities of similar worth as those through the sale of which the money was obtained.

Confidence or faith in money is crucial, because by itself, money has no real value. That used to be the case even in the time when the value of a coin was reflected in its gold or silver contents. After all, gold and silver are intrinsically worthless: neither of these metals has much practical use. Like any metal, they are unfit for human consumption, and they are too malleable to make any useful tools. The intrinsic value of paper money (bank notes or bills) is even less than that of coins. That was why for a long time its value was guaranteed by gold reserves, held at the bank that issued the bills. With the enormous growth of the global economy, however, the principle of backing up the nominal value of all newly issued money with gold has been impossible to maintain. Now, the value of currencies depends more than ever on the faith people put in it.

On closer examination, doesn't it seem odd that the lack of this artificial, symbolic object that is so often mentioned as the main limitation for addressing the world's problems? If it were lack of natural resources, of labor, or of skills and knowledge, the difficulty would be understandable: changing any of these factors overnight is beyond our capacity. But being nothing more than a concept money can, in principle, be created or destroyed at will. Most of the money going round in the world today does not even exist physically: it does not take the form of either coins or paper money. It only appears in 'the books' or, nowadays, the memory chips of computers. Therefore, in creating it there is not even the physical limitation of the capacity of the world's printing presses. A simple statement by the financial authorities should, in principle, be sufficient to create any amount of money.

The fact that today money can be created at will is an important development. In the past the capacity for money creation was limited by the availability of gold and silver—either as a component of the alloys used for coins, or as backing for bank notes issued by banks. If rulers did not dispose of gold and silver they could borrow from those who did. But they could not produce money out of thin air and have it maintain its value. Today, governments can, and do. In countries with stable, internationally accepted currencies money is created by a Central Bank (or a central banking system, such as the Federal Reserve in the U.S.). As a rule, it does so when commercial banks solicit capital to cover the credit needs of their clients. This is the generally accepted basis for money creation. Underlying this principle is a deep faith in the infallibility of the market: if from the many economic actors who make up the market there arises a demand for money, there must be an economic need for it.

Whereas banks can turn to the Central Bank if they need money and thus, can solicit money creation, a government cannot. Governments who do are looked upon with disdain by the international financial community, and their currencies are not internationally accepted. Such acceptance is reserved only for governments who borrow the funds they lack from the private sector. Today, such loans are obtained in national and international capital markets through the issue of bonds.

There are two things wrong with this form of financing. The first is that banks can borrow money from the Central Bank at a lower interest rate than that which the state has to pay on the bonds it issues. That's a sweet deal for the banks: they can borrow at a low rate, buy bonds that will pay a significantly higher rate, and pocket the difference. Thus, the system constantly subsidizes commercial banks which, of course, are privately owned. Those who pay for these subsidies are, obviously, the taxpayers.

The second problem with government borrowing in capital markets is that money is borrowed on commercial terms for financing non-commercial activities. In case of a commercial loan, money is borrowed to invest in something that is expected to yield a sufficiently high return to pay back the loan plus interest and make a profit. The areas in which government operates, though, are not commercial. Education, health care, law enforcement, environmental protection and building roads and bridges are important, but they don't usually earn enough money to pay for themselves. In the few cases where they do, mainstream economists and politicians immediately call for privatization: if a profit can be made, the activity is commercial, and if it's commercial, it should be turned over to the private sector.

Thus, the state—and therefore, the citizenry—gets a raw deal. It is not allowed to engage in profitable ventures, yet when it needs to borrow money it must do so on commercial terms. Small wonder, then, that both the rich and the poor nations have gotten themselves deeply into debt.

Today, as we've seen, the limits of borrowing by the state have come in sight. Debt servicing takes up huge parts of national budgets. As a result, there is no money left for the large-scale investment needed to finance sustainable development. Therefore, sustainable development should be financed in ways that do not increase the public debt. That can be achieved by making the needed money directly available to the state, without first channeling it through banks and financial markets.

Money creation and inflation

The taboo against creating money for use by the government stems from the fear of inflation. There is good reason for this concern. History is rife with examples of governments engaging in large-scale money creation for their own use. Almost always, this form of money creation led to high inflation. In some cases hyperinflation occurred, with currencies' values being decimated by the day.

Creating money for use by the state, therefore, is not without risk. But that's no reason to disqualify the practice altogether—even though economists will do so out of hand. They'll argue that today, thanks to policies that let the market decide on money creation, the supply of money and that of goods and services are balanced. If the state creates money for its own use, this balance would be upset: there would be too much money. According to the law of supply and demand, where there is excess, the price will drop. That means the value of money would decrease relative to that of goods and services. In other words: prices would rise, and you'd have inflation.

The error in this assumption is that it mixes micro-economic with macro-economic phenomena. It assumes that decision making by individuals and companies on price setting (the field of micro-economics) has direct consequences for prices in the economy as a whole (the area of macro-economics). But in today's complex society, producers have no insight at all on how the total amount of money circulating in the economy affects the price they can ask for their product. When producers lower or raise prices, they do not have their eye on the total money supply. Instead, they look at the competition, at consumer behavior, and at predictions on how the market will develop.

Another error is that the theory on the relationship between the money supply and inflation is based on a closed economy. With millions of dollars in money and goods crossing borders every minute, that condition hardly applies.

The fact that considerable increases in the money supply do not necessarily cause inflation is easily illustrated. Look at the money that is created through speculation in the private sector. Hundreds of billions of dollars were generated in the booms in stock markets and real estate in the 1980s, particularly in the U.S. and Japan. Yet in spite of this enormous infusion in the economy, inflation did not rise significantly. Why not? Partly, because an important proportion of this extra capital was not used to purchase goods and services, but for further speculation. Thus, demand did not grow in proportion to the increase in the money supply. The most important factor in checking inflation, though, was that since the money was created in the (financial) market, people did not lose faith in its value. After all, the market can't be wrong. Which goes to show that, as long as faith is maintained (in this case, through the blind trust in the 'infallible hand' of the market) money can, in principle, be created at will without causing inflation.

The 'in principle' is an important qualification. Because when money creation generates so much demand that it cannot be met by producers, they'll take notice and raise their prices. Likewise, when workers find there is more demand for their services than they offer, they're likely to raise *their* price by demanding higher wages. In both cases, inflation *will* result. The conclusion, then, is that as long as money created for the state is not used in ways that generate more demand than can be satisfied by producers, inflation can be avoided.

Money creation for use by the state would violate one of the most sacred dogmas of the financial community. Still, even some economic and financial specialists appear to recognize that adding money to the world's capital supply is feasible even without the private sector demanding it. Thus, money creation for use by the state was recently proposed by none other than the director of the International Monetary Fund—one of the greatest bastions of conservative economics. In 1994, it requested permission of its shareholders to create an additional $60 billion in so-called Special Drawing Rights: money that can be borrowed by the governments of member nations. Only a fraction of this amount—some $15 billion—was actually approved by the dominant shareholders, the rich nations. Especially the German Central Bank objected to creating new SDRs. The reason was, obviously, fear of inflation.[1] Nevertheless, an agreement for what amounts to money creation for the state was reached—even though the amount involved was small. This fact, as well as the original request made by the IMF director, indicates that the *principle* of money creation is not as farfetched as it may seem.

Avoiding demand-driven inflation

Now let's assume that the principle of money creation for the state is accepted. The question then becomes how to go about it without causing inflation. One cause of inflation would be that the a program for sustainable development would generate so much demand that producers would feel free to raise their prices at will. That would cause what economists call demand-pull inflation. Also, such excessive demand could lead to producers competing for labor, capital goods and raw materials. That would push up the prices of all three, and therefore, the prices of the products made by and with them. That's called cost-push inflation. Both could occur if demand by the state would outstrip the capacity of the economy to produce the desired goods and services. To avoid this, demand by the state should be adapted to existing production capacity. That means that programs paid for through money creation should aim to use the economy's unused or underutilized production potential.

FIGURE 2 *Utilization of production capacity: at present and in a situation of money creation for sustainable development*

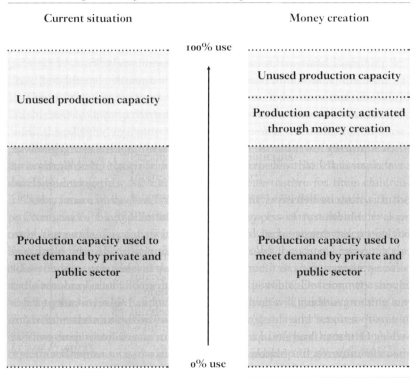

As a rule, there is enough opportunity to do so. In a recession, as little as 70% of the production capacity of the economy may be in use. Even in a full recovery as much as 15% of production capacity may remain unused.[2] However, public investment financed by money creation should not lay claim to all unused production capacity. In no economy is production capacity ever fully attuned to demand: part of the unused workers and capital goods are accommodated to making goods and services other than those that are wanted. Moreover, if all production capacity is used there will be little or no competition between suppliers, which leads to higher prices and less efficiency. To maintain competition, therefore, only part of the underutilized production capacity should be used (Figure 2).

Governments should actively foster the expansion of the country's production capacity for goods and services that, once a program for sustainable development would be set in motion, would prove to be in short supply. New schools, colleges and universities should be created, and the training and research capacity of existing institutions expanded. Tax breaks and where needed, financing should be supplied for investments in research for increasing productivity and a more efficient use of scarce production inputs.

By having producers compete for contracts, the market could be given a key role in attuning money creation to production capacity. With insufficient participation and all contenders charging exorbitant fees, the state should assume that production capacity were stretched to the limit. The program involved should then be reduced in size or postponed, until a sufficient number of competitors would offer to do the job at reasonable cost.

Avoiding inflation through loss of faith

If money creation would make financial markets lose their faith in a currency, its value would diminish. To keep the faith, an international approach would be needed, in which all or a majority of nations with strong currencies would accept and actually engage in money creation for sustainable development. If this were not the case, currency traders, mindful of economic dogma, would be likely to get rid of currencies in which money would be created, and buy those in which it wouldn't. That would reduce the value of currencies of countries engaging in money creation. Money managers would withdraw their capital from the local stock market, and serious economic and financial trouble would ensue.

No country would want to risk that. Therefore, the mandate to create money should not be given to national Central Banks. Instead it should remain with an independent, international agency that enjoys the confidence of financial markets. Such an agency already exists: the IMF.

The IMF could provide funding for sustainable development with something comparable to the already mentioned Special Drawing Rights. Let's call these new units 'Allotments for Sustainable Investment', or ASIS. ASIS would be different from SDRs in two ways. SDRs involve loans at commercial interest rates, and can be used as the receiving nation sees fit. ASIS, however, would not require repayment, and would be disbursed only for investment in sustainable development.

ASI disbursements should be made dependent on several conditions. First, with the help of specialists from relevant national and international organizations, IMF experts should judge if a request for ASI financing would indeed concern an investment in sustainable development. Second, the IMF would have to assess the risks of demand-pull and cost-push inflation. If the activities to be financed would make too high a demand on existing production capacity, the IMF should demand rescheduling. Third, the IMF should only approve ASI disbursements for activities that would be part of a national program for sustainable development. This program should define all activities to be undertaken in the different fields of sustainable development. It should establish priorities, according to the availability of the human and material resources needed to carry out the activities. Also, the program should define monetary, fiscal and economic policies aimed at controlling inflation and balancing government budgets. Particularly for poor countries this should include measures for creating a solid tax base, through progressive taxation and the stringent enforcement of tax laws.

Follow-up requests for ASI financing should be honored only if the already allotted funds were spent for the uses for which it was intended. Moreover, disbursement of ASIS should, in principle, be conditioned on adherence to the principles of democratic government. The reason would be, even more than moral, practical: accountability. Without freedom of information, organization, and an independent judiciary, it would be difficult to hold a government responsible for the misuse of ASI funding.

The condition of democratic government should, however, be managed with some flexibility. Some ASI financed programs might benefit large numbers of people even though their government would not be democratic. That could be the case with programs aimed at education, health care, poverty alleviation and natural resource management. Carried out by a reasonable effective civil service, such programs could contribute enormously to sustainable development. Moreover, improved education would contribute to fostering democracy in the countries involved.

Whenever possible programs and projects financed through ASIS should aim to become self-sustaining. That is, after the initial investment, they should yield sufficient benefits to cover all costs. That would be the case particularly for projects aimed at stimulating production, such as roads and bridges, land improvement, and water supply. After having received ASI financing for the initial investment, all costs for operation, maintenance and replacement should be covered in the normal way: through user fees, taxes, and the project's economic proceeds.

Repeated ASI contributions should be reserved exclusively for programs that would not yield direct benefits, and would require support over longer periods of time rather than a major initial investment. Examples would be programs for education, health care, ecosystem management and the pension and child support funds described in Chapter VI. Here also, though, ASI financing would be temporary, to be replaced gradually with regular funding. All ASI agreements would have to include a timetable for this substitution.

ASIS could also be used to pay back the interest and principal on national debts. This would free government resources for more productive uses. The idea would not be to pay off all debts in one move: an injection that size into capital markets would create financial chaos. Rather, ASIS for debt servicing would be issued according to existing repayment schedules.

ASIS for debt relief should be tied to the obligation for the beneficiary governments to balance their budgets. Even better would be if governments created some reserves for contingencies, such as natural disasters and downturns in the business cycle—when due to stagnating economic growth revenues drop and spending on social security rises. Creating such reserves would call for budget surpluses in years with sturdy economic growth.

The IMF should not honor requests for money creation if, in the country involved, inflation would be on the rise. Rising inflation could be caused by excessive wage demands from workers, or by producers raising prices. Thus, money creation would be dependent not only on the responsible behavior of governments, but also on that of employers and workers. All parties involved should come to see that avoiding inflation would be in their own best interest. Workers and their unions should understand that moderate wage demands, linked to gains in productivity, would not only maintain the value of their pay, but also keep their country eligible for ASI financing of new projects and programs. Similarly, producers should realize that reasonable profit margins, gained over a number of years and high turnover, would yield more than high profits for a short period, on lesser volumes. If a majority of workers and employers could be convinced of these benefits, unions, business and government could create a climate in which sustained money creation for sustainable development would become possible.

Obviously, governments would also profit handsomely from money creation. Sustained, sustainable economic growth would generate more jobs, wealth and overall well-being. The result: a satisfied electorate. More jobs and economic growth would also mean more tax revenues. In the longer run, this might allow the lowering of taxes, making voters even happier. For all parties involved, then, financing sustainable development through careful money creation would provide obvious benefits and thus, incentives to behave responsibly.

Local money creation

ASIs would be created at the international level, by a global financial institute. However, money can also be created at the other end of the scale: at the local level. The use of local currency can stimulate local economies by fostering the production, exchange and consumption of goods and services within the community. This is already happening today: since the early 1980s several hundred communities, mostly in Australia, Ireland, England and North America, have initiated so-called Financial Micro-Initiatives, or FMIs.[3]

The local money created through FMIs exists side by side with national currencies. Its economic effects are particularly strong in places where national currency is in short supply, such as areas with high unemployment. There are also environmental advantages: satisfaction of individual and communal needs will take place more sustainably if decisions on the use of local resources are taken within the community. Locals are more likely to use their natural resources rationally than outsiders, who tend to come in, exploit and move on. Moreover, since production and consumption take place in the same locality, transport needs are minimal, which saves non-renewable energy. Thus, economic activity resulting from FMIs is as a rule more environment-friendly than that financed by regular money.[4]

Local money is, of course, nothing new. In fact, money first appeared at the local level: in villages, towns and cities. The dominance of national currencies is typical only of the last century; the world-wide acceptance of a single means of exchange, the dollar, is more recent still. This international-ization of money has contributed greatly to the free movement of capital across borders. In turn, this has led to the growing concentration of the global capital supply in international financial centers, at the cost of economically less favored places. In poor countries and in 'pockets' of poverty in rich ones, the lack of regular money and consequently, demand, depresses economies. To counter this requires a return to our financial roots: the payment for com-munity produced goods and services with local currency.

A remarkable example of local money creation is that of the small island of Guernsey, situated between England and France. Between 1816 and 1829 a total of 48,000 'States Notes' were issued, each with a face value of one English pound. At a time of deep economic crisis, they were used to finance sorely needed public works such as roads, a market place, schools and sea defenses. The resulting demand for skilled and unskilled labor and raw ma-terials greatly helped in pulling the island out of its economic depression. In later years more States notes were issued; today, some 14 million pounds worth of notes and coins circulate side-by-side with the English pound.

The U.S. also has a long history of local money creation. At the height of the Great Depression, in 1933, more than 300 communities, mostly in the Mid-West and North-East, used local currencies. However in March 1933 President F.D. Roosevelt, answering to pressure from national financial authorities who feared they would loose control over monetary policy, for-bade further issues. A similar fate struck many FMIs that in the early 20th century appeared in Europe, especially in Scandinavia and Germany. Here also, national financial authorities feared loss of control over the money sup-ply and consequently, inflation.

Today FMIs are once again gaining popularity. Most of these initiatives do not actually involve the physical creation and use of a local currency. Instead measuring units, such as hours of work, are earned, registered in a local banking system, and spent on locally produced goods and services. FMI members are issued chequebooks and receive regular statements of account through a computer based cheque clearing system. Since no actual money is involved, it's a system with which even the most orthodox financial author-ities will find it hard to find fault.

FMIs, then, are both complementary to, and offer an antidote for today's growing concentration of capital. They are an alternative that becomes all the more important when one takes into account that whereas FMIs are already operating today, capital creation through ASIs is still a long way off.

A new economics

Money creation would be important even without a program for sustainable development. That is because at some point, money creation without taking on debt will become necessary. The reason, as was discussed throughout this book, is that for economic growth to be sustained, increasing productivity must be matched by an increase in demand. The market is unable to generate this increase. In the past two decades, demand has held its own largely because of deficit financing, in the private as well as the public sector. With humanity now deeper in debt than ever before, the limits to this strategy have come in sight. A radically new approach to economic development is therefore needed: money creation through ASIs and, at the local level, FMIs.

ASIs would eliminate chronic budget deficits and create the demand for goods and services that is needed to close the growing gap between productivity and demand. Increased demand would also limit the competitive rat race that now results in declining living standards for all but the top layers of society. Moreover, by creating investment opportunities in the productive sector of the economy, money creation for sustainable development could curb the concentration of capital in the international financial markets. That would reduce speculation and thus, diminish the chance of a financial crash.

The idea of money creation, then, should not only be seen as a way to help finance sustainable development. It should also be considered as a first step to adapting economic thought to today's realities. What we need is a new economics, which will enable us to satisfy the world's needs by developing and utilizing its productive potential as efficiently as possible.

This need becomes all the more urgent when we consider the enormous progress that has been made, in the past few decades, in technology and the natural sciences. In stark contrast, economics is still mired in theories developed in the 19th century. Today's economists apply these theories to today's situation as if they were universal and timeless truths. As a result society's productive capacity is increasingly oriented towards the satisfaction, often in unsustainable ways, of the demands of the already well-off. Simultaneously, the needs of the poor and of future generations go unanswered.

Instead of being used for the benefit of all of humanity, then, technology serves only the needs of those able to pay for it. Much technology that could greatly contribute to sustainable development is not or insufficiently exploited because according to traditional economic reckoning, it's 'uneconomical' to do so. Economic policies based on outdated or false assumptions help to widen the gap between have's and have-not's, contributing to continued mass unemployment and poverty. And we're only at the beginning: as things are going, we're in for more human misery, a major economic and financial crisis, and a seriously disrupted global ecosystem. What's needed, therefore, is a new approach to economics, with as its central question how to use society's resources to optimally satisfy humanity's needs in the short, medium and long run.

Part 4

STRATEGY

'Needed changes will only come about as the expression of the political will of peoples in many parts of the world.'

Olof Palme, former Prime Minister of Sweden

Chapter XIII

THE MOVEMENT

At the end of Chapter X it was concluded that there is little chance that to-day's politicians will put us on the road to sustainable development. They lack the vision, morals, backbone and daring to attempt to change things around. Caught up in the hierarchy of interests described in Chapter V, they'll continue to defend their own short term, local interests and those of their constituencies, at the expense of the long term common good.

To generate the radical change that is needed, we'll need an approach that can break through today's political logjam. The core of that approach is the creation of a worldwide movement. Its objective should be to elaborate a global program for sustainable development, and to generate enough support for it to be implemented. This global program should form the basis for regional pro-grams (for example, North America, Europe, the Middle East) and national plans. For large nations, consisting of federations of states with heterogeneous populations and resources, 'zonal' or 'state' plans should be elaborated. As the movement would develop, plans should also be made for the local level.

Thus, a hierarchy of programs would be created. At the top would be the global plan, followed, in descending order, by the regional, national, zonal and local programs. The key trait of this hierarchy would be that each pro-gram would fit into the program at the level above.

All programs—global, regional, national and zonal—should offer an inte-grated approach to all the issues related to sustainable development: from the economy to the environment, from education to health care to social security, and from law enforcement and taxation to political issues such as local and regional autonomy. Also, they should give indications of how and when dif-ferent program components should be carried out, their approximate cost, their economic effects, and ways of financing.

The vertical links between programs imply that changes at one level would have consequences at other levels. Especially higher level programs should therefore not be detailed blueprints but frameworks, to be worked out in more detail at lower levels. The filling in of these broad sketches should happen 'on the ground', with people and their legitimate representatives at the national, zonal and local level. Also, the framework model would facilitate the adaptation of programs to changes in social, economic and technological conditions.

The global plan for sustainable development should be formulated by an interdisciplinary team of specialists in such fields as ecology, land use, energy, education, health care, economics, public administration, law, and international relations. All 'program developers' should, in addition to their own specialty, be generalists: they should have a basic idea of the main concepts and methods of other areas of expertise. This general body of knowledge would form the basis for successful cooperation between all team members.

Obviously, the team members should be in agreement with the general concept of the need for a worldwide, integrated approach towards sustainable development. They should be pragmatic, that is, practically oriented and not tied to specific dogmas, ideologies or schools of thought. These traits would allow them to consider, analyze and adapt any reasonable options for sustainable development—independent of their source, or their degree of conformity with existing ideas. In particular, program makers should be flexible enough to change their point of view when presented with convincing arguments to do so. That would allow for incorporating new ideas that, after thorough analysis, would appear to present a better approach to solving specific problems than the strategy proposed up-to-then.

Although this sounds reasonable enough, today such attitudes are the exception rather than the rule. Politicians, opinion leaders, even scientists tend to defend their standpoints, beliefs, and theories for better or for worse. Drawing them into question is often considered a personal insult. Discussions are not based on a well-considered analysis of the arguments, but on proclamations and attempts to cast doubt on the integrity of the opponent. Such attitudes will not help the drive for sustainable development. What is needed, instead, is an attitude that considers a thoroughly argued critique as a challenge to refine ideas and proposals.

The global program team should be at the center of a network of teams responsible for the regional, national and zonal programs. All these teams should consist of a core of permanent members, to which external experts could be added temporarily to work on specific themes. Where needed, experts from the global and regional teams should assist in the formulation of lower-level programs. Vice versa, representatives of lower level teams could be delegated temporarily to higher level teams. Thus, the compatibility of lower level plans with higher level ones could be ensured.

Although knowledge of and experience with scientific methods would be important, program developers should also be able to take some distance from academic standards. This more pragmatic approach would be needed in cases where urgent problems would require the rapid development of programs. Decisions would then have to be taken on the basis of the available knowledge, even though from a scientific point of view such knowledge might not be sufficient to draw firm conclusions. Program developers should not be concerned about the possible loss of academic status that could result.

Participation in the program development teams should not be limited to scientists. In principle, anyone with a record of well-reasoned and creative publications in a relevant area of expertise should be eligible. Applicants for a team position should be judged less on their titles and Curriculum Vitae than on their ability to express, orally and especially on paper, analyses, ideas and courses of action relevant for program development.

The Global Future Network

All teams, including the global team, should be employed by a worldwide network of organizations. Let's call this the Global Future Network, GFN. The core of this network would be the GFN headquarters, where the global program would be worked out. In line with the above described hierarchy there would also be regional, national, zonal and local GFN branches.

GFN headquarters would have to be established in a politically stable and democratically governed nation. The locale should have good communications and an acceptable cost of living—the latter, to avoid high overhead costs. Headquarters as well as the regional, national and zonal branches would have departments covering all fields of sustainable development: natural resource management, land use, energy, economics, political science, education, child development, public administration, law, criminology and health care. A special coordinating unit should integrate the plans worked out in the different departments into a general program.

Regional offices should be created for groups of countries with comparable social and economic traits. Like the seat of headquarters, they should be established in democratic, politically stable countries with good communications. They should be staffed with specialists from the region itself, liaisons from headquarters, and representatives from the national branches of the region involved.

National GFN offices should be established in every country where it would be possible to operate without political persecution. In the case of political obstacles in a certain country, the staff of the national GFN office for that country should be situated at the regional center. As said, in large nations, consisting of ecologically, economically, politically and culturally heterogeneous regions and populations, zonal branches should be created.

The elaboration of the global, regional and national programs for sustainable development should not start from scratch. On the contrary, as much use as possible should be made of the enormous reservoir of already existing knowledge, information, ideas, plans and proposals. In most countries, hosts of organizations, many of them non-governmental, are engaged in research and action concerning the environment, poverty, education, health care, and other fields relevant for sustainable development. GFN program teams should actively seek the cooperation of these organizations, and incorporate their knowledge and experience into program formulation. Ideas and proposals should be analyzed, and adapted to and integrated with other relevant program components. As far as possible, changes should be worked out with the organizations concerned. That would allow the use of their expertise, and establish a basis for future cooperation. The ideal result of such exchanges would be the mutual acceptance and endorsement of each other's programs and policies, as well as mutual support for the attempts to get those programs and policies implemented.

Apart from the expertise present in established organizations there is also an enormous reservoir of ideas among individuals. People from all walks of life have valuable experience and knowledge that could support the drive for sustainable development. Over the years, many of these people have developed proposals to address specific social, economic or political problems. Most have never been implemented. Usually, this was because they went against vested interests, in other cases, the reason was the general inertia of bureaucracies. The GFN should provide such people and groups with an outlet for their ideas and proposals. Thus, their experience, knowledge and creative energy could be used to strengthen national, regional and global programs.

Although developing the programs would be the first priority, GFN staff should also, on request, advise governments, government institutions and non-governmental organizations on policies for sustainable development.

Such advice should, obviously, be based on the GFN programs worked out for the countries involved. As a rule GFN staff should not, however, take direct responsibility for carrying out specific development programs or projects. Exceptions could be made for pilot projects to test out strategies proposed by the GFN—for example, the CHEC concept proposed in Chapter VII. Broader involvement in project execution would be justified only when this would not involve draining human and financial resources from GFN core activities.

To become a movement, the GFN should develop a membership. To have an impact, that membership should be large: the larger, the better. Publicity campaigns should bring the GFN and its ideas to people's attention, and get them involved. The key challenge would be to generate a response from the lower income groups and the poor, in both rich and poor countries. Since these groups are not as a rule avid readers—in poor countries, a significant proportion is illiterate—radio and television would be key means for publicity. Besides communicating its views in print, the GFN should therefore also aim to set up its own radio and television network.

Just presenting people with the notion of sustainable development and the plans to bring it about would be unlikely to foster real enthusiasm. To become and remain motivated, the long-term perspective on a better world would have to be complemented by concrete benefits and advice that could help people improve their lives immediately. For example, in poor countries recommendations could be given on such topics as sustainable agriculture and gardening, setting up small enterprises, nutrition, and family health. Also, in rich as well as poor nations, information could be given on consumer products, government services, the political situation, and cultural activities. Special educational programs could be provided for children of all ages. To keep the attention of listeners and viewers, educational and informative programs should be varied with entertainment.

The programming of the GFN radio and TV stations, and the contents of written media, should therefore be innovative, combining to the extent possible information supply with entertainment and educational elements. The financing for these media could be obtained partially by advertising products whose use would be in line with sustainable development. Additional funding could be obtained from subscriptions and general GFN membership fees.

Another GFN activity would be to collect information and process it into readily usable handbooks and guides. Today, there is an enormous mass of scientific and other literature, on every imaginable subject. The problem is to select, from this heap of information, the most relevant materials. Literature searches easily yield hundreds or even thousands of titles, available in libraries all over the world. For most people, particularly in poor countries, all this literature is difficult or costly to access. Even those specializing in providing information to others don't have the time to work through all the available information to get what they need. Therefore, experiences and knowledge are insufficiently shared. As a result, effective ways to handle problems are not disseminated, and avoidable errors are made many times over, at different moments in different places. The GFN could help resolve this problem by selecting, for all themes related to sustainable development, the most relevant theoretical, methodological and practical insights, and present them in easy-to-use guides. These should be updated regularly to include the most recently acquired knowledge and information. Fields to be covered would be, among others, education and pedagogy, basic health care and sanitation, sustainable agriculture, natural resource management, poverty alleviation, public administration, law enforcement, and criminology.

Such sustainable development guides should be made available at minimal cost to every interested party. Also, they would come to serve as the basis for teaching and training programs, in special GFN training centers and possibly, schools and universities. Such learning institutions should provide complete curricula for degrees, as well as shorter courses in fields related to sustainable development. The centers could be newly created or, where feasible, based on joint ventures with existing schools and universities.

The GFN should also aim to improve the curricula for regular education. Emphasis should be put on mental development and learning for the very young, and on integrating subjects such as civics, ecology and health in existing curricula. Another focal point would be the development and promotion of teaching methods and materials that would enhance the analytical and problem solving skills of students.

A final field of activity of the GFN would be to help organizations already engaging in activities related to sustainable development. As was mentioned concerning assistance to governments, the GFN should not as a rule initiate its own programs, projects and activities at field level, with the exception of pilot projects to try out new approaches. However, it should support nongovernmental organizations and government agencies known to operate effectively in such fields as natural resource management and poverty alleviation. Such support could consist of funding, information supply, and training. To ensure adequate spending as well as maximum effectiveness, the GFN should regularly assess and evaluate such programs.

As a non governmental organization, the GFN should be financed through private contributions. People sympathizing with GFN ideas and principles should be encouraged to become contributing members. The minimum contribution could be set at an amount that would cover the costs of administration and information transfer via a GFN publication. For funding the activities described in the above, bigger donations would be required. These could be made dependent on income: for example, a contribution of 0.1% of a member's gross income could be suggested as a voluntary guideline. Donating higher percentages should of course be encouraged.

GFNs could also raise funds by engaging in income generating activities related to sustainable development. Examples would be advising governments and development organizations, and advertising in GFN owned media. Also, those able to pay should be charged fees for education, training and other services. Moreover, GFN members could be offered products and services that, while making membership more attractive, would also generate additional revenues: gifts, clothing, media products such as educational books and videos, and possibly, selected consumer products and travel.

The GFN, then, should develop into a large, multi-layered and -faceted organization. Good management would be essential to its functioning. At all levels, dynamic, creative, experienced and dedicated staff should take care of daily management, planning and strategy formulation. Management at each level should be checked by a council consisting of representatives from the level below. Thus, the global management team would be checked by a council consisting of representatives from the regional branches. This council assembly should meet regularly, say once or twice a year, to evaluate the GFNs progress and discuss and take decisions on important issues such as key appointments. Also, it should approve the global and regional development programs. For closer tabs on and support for the GFN management, the council should select a board. This board could consist of five representatives, one for each continent: America, Europe, Africa, Asia and Australia/Oceania.

Obviously, all council and board members, as well as the GFN management, should have an untainted reputation of intellectual and political integrity, both in their country of origin and internationally. Also, they should have the same intellectual flexibility, that is, they should be as pragmatic, as open to reasonable arguments, and as averse to dogmatism as was suggested for the rest of the GFN staff.

If the global movement described in the above would come about as described, it would become a very powerful organization. But power corrupts: even the most well-intentioned and capable persons are, when given too much power for too long, tempted to abuse it. One way to avoid this would be the careful selection of staff. To ensure their integrity to the extent possible, candidates for leading positions should, in addition to having un untainted reputation, provide a complete disclosure of their personal wealth and its origins, and proof of full compliance with the tax laws of their nation.

Another, even more important guarantee against abuse of power would be for the movement to develop its own system of checks and balances. The above mentioned council would be a key element in checking GFN management and professional staff at the global level. At the other levels, regional, national and local councils would be created with similar functions. As said, at regional, national and state levels these councils would be formed by representatives from lower levels. At the local level, the councils would be elected directly by GFN members.

Another component of the checks and balances system would be a sort of judiciary, consisting of Arbitration Boards. The role of these boards, to be formed at all levels, would be to ensure that GFN program proposals and operational procedures would correspond to the principles of sustainable development. To be able to do so they would need a charter, that is, a sort of constitution that would define those principles. Drawing up this charter should be one of the first things the movement should do. However, as with any constitution, it should be possible to adapt the charter to changing circumstances and new insights. This task should fall to the global council, which should be given the power to change the Charter with a three-quarter majority.

Whenever needed, that is to say, whenever members of the executive branch or the council would request it, the Arbitration Board should come into action. In case of a negative verdict, the proposal or action involved would have to be reformulated, withdrawn or canceled. Thus, the movement's compliance with the principles of sustainable development, in its programs as well as its actions, would to the extent possible be ensured.

The Global Future Party

Now, let's assume the GFN would be created, and would elaborate its programs, build up its membership, and develop its information network and other services. To actually bring about change, it would then have to strive for the implementation of the programs. Of course a strong GFN, with a large membership spread over many countries, could wield significant political influence. However, to obtain direct political power would require the formation of a political party, which should aim to rise to power via the ballot box. Let's call this the Global Future Party, or GFP.

As there is no such thing as a global government to take over, the GFP should seek political power at the national level. That would call for the formation of as many GFPs as there are nations. Yet GFPs would differ from traditional political parties. In the latter, programs, if existing at all, are elaborated by politicians and their staff. The GFP, on the other hand, would base its political goals on the GFN programs. Thus, in each nation there would be a close partnership between GFN and GFP, with the first responsible for program development, and the second for its implementation.

Another way in which the GFP would differ from existing political parties would be that, because of its structure and mode of operation, it would avoid the problems affecting politics today. By adopting the same structure as the GFP, with an executive branch, a council with legislative and controlling functions, and an arbitration board operating on the basis of a charter, it would ensure the democratic representation of its members in decision making, adherence to the principles of sustainable development, and the integrity of its officials and representatives. Thus, the back room wheeling and dealing, the influence peddling of special interests, and the power plays based on money and favors that mark most of today's political parties would be avoided. Also, these checks and balances would ensure, to the extent possible, the integrity of GFP politicians. Moreover, because of the GFNs watchdog function, politicians would be bound to their election time promises.

At the core of the GFP charter should be the principle of striving to carry out the national, regional and global GFN programs. However, the GFP would operate at the national level and thus, be subject to international forces over which it would have little or no control. Moreover, it would be unlikely that even at the national level, a GFP would immediately gain the absolute majority needed to carry out is program. In practice, therefore, it would be necessary for the GFP to adapt the GFN program to national and international political and economic realities. Such adaptation would carry the risk that, under the influence of the same forces that now impede sustainable development, GFP programs would be watered down too much. To avoid this, changes in the contents or actual implementation of GFP programs would have to be made dependent on detailed consultation and approval by the GFN. In other words, GFP programs and strategy would have to be ratified by the GFN, so as to ensure they'd remain in line with national, regional and global GFN programs.

In comparison with traditional politics, there would be three great advantages to the intimate link between the GFP, as a political party, and the GFN as the developer of its program. The first would be clarity about the political program. The public would be presented with a clear-cut program for the short, medium and long term. In contrast, today most mainstream political parties have only very vague programs, or don't have any at all. Thus, voters would obtain a much clearer picture of what their party would stand for. ˙

The second advantage of the GFN-GFP link would be that the GFP, as a political party, would be under constant scrutiny from an independent entity: the GFN. That would put much greater pressure on the GFP to stick to its program than would be the case for normal political parties. In traditional politics, such scrutiny hardly exists, making it easy for politicians to say one thing and do another. The GFN-GFP relationship, however, would provide voters with an easy check on the reliability of politicians. If the GFN would maintain its endorsement, GFP politicians could be assumed to have stuck to the extent possible to their commitments. Withdrawal of the endorsement would mean politicians had gone wrong.

The third, and greatest advantage of the GFP-GFN link would be the potential for effective international cooperation. Through the programmatic ties between national, regional and global GFNs, all national GFPs would have compatible programs. GFP politicians would be in basic agreement regarding the way international problems should be addressed: the solutions would already form part of the regional and global GFN programs. This kind of unity of purpose, and clarity on how to address global problems, would be the basis for genuine international cooperation, and break the logjam that marks today's efforts to address the world's problems.

Some may argue that today, there already are worldwide organizations of political parties, comparable to the proposed GFP network. They are right in that international federations of, for example, social democrats, conservatives, socialists and Christian Democrats indeed exist. But these federations are no more than loose networks of parties which, although based on the same political-philosophical concept, have their own history and characteristics. Practically any party pretending to adhere to that concept is allowed to join—even though the actions of the politicians involved have little relationship to that concept. At best, then, such organizations may unite to further their common political interest: to obtain or stay in power. But they don't contribute much to real cooperation and integration, and even less to a coherent approach to global development.

So what's the chance that GFPs might actually attract the interest of voters? Over the last decade, voter dissatisfaction with existing political parties and politicians has risen to unprecedented highs. Therefore, there is considerable potential for a new political party such as the GFP. The public could come to appreciate a party that does not to focus on serving itself and special interests, but sticks to a set of clearly defined policies for the common good. Much would depend on the ability of GFN and GFP to translate the idea of sustainable development into a clear message with which the interest of voters could be aroused. If that message could activate part of those still politically active as well as those who, over the last decade, have turned their back on politics, the potential would be enormous.

To become a credible alternative for existing political parties, the GFPs would need, in addition to a clear program, credible and inspired leadership. As with the GFN, its candidates and representatives should be untainted by any sort of scandal; to ensure this, they should be willing and able to give complete disclosure of their financial situation and the ways their wealth was obtained. Under those conditions, the GFP could also open itself to 'traditional' politicians: experienced, well known, but scrupulous politicians should be drawn aboard. Similarly, existing political parties with agendas not too far removed from GFN programs should be encouraged to evolve into *de facto* GFPs.

A major risk for GFPs and GFNs would be political compromise. If GFNs and GFPs were to come off the ground, and a GFP would actually receive a large proportion of votes, it might have to enter some kind of power sharing arrangement with other political parties. That would require compromises, which should be clearly explained to voters. Also, GFPs would have to adjust to economic, political and financial realities at the international level. For example, the introduction of an environmental tax that would double the price of oil would be hard to realize in only one country, as it would put business there at too great a disadvantage. Similarly, certain fiscal measures might cause money managers to withdraw funds from the country involved, causing economic and financial problems. Such realities should lead the national, regional and global GFN to apply the necessary flexibility when endorsing a national GFP. As long as the GFN-GFP coalition would not be able to influence the global *status quo* decisively, GFPs and GFN would have to adapt to it.

Cooperation for sustainable development

Let's fantasize some more, and assume a number of countries would actually come to be governed by GFPs. To foster sustainable development, such nations should then develop special cooperative relationships. Thus, rich GFP countries should focus their development assistance on poor GFP counterparts. In line with sustainable development, such aid should focus on health care, education, natural resource management, and public service reform. Assistance could also be given in the improvement of the transportation and communications infrastructure. Moreover, special trade relationships should be developed, through the formation of a free trade bloc. Within it, obstacles to the free flow of goods, services, and capital should be removed gradually. In line with the principles of sustainable development, trade should, however, be based on a bottom line, so as to protect the environment, workers and consumers.

Trade between GFP nations and non-GFP countries could take place on the basis of a system of differential trade relations, much as the U.S. and the European Community already use today. The 'most favored', 'lesser favored' and 'least favored' status should be assigned according to the degree to which the nations involved would adhere to the principles of sustainable development. For example, a country paying considerable attention to education, health care and the management of its natural resources, and with a fairly democratic government, would receive a most-favored status. On the other hand, a nation headed by a dictatorial regime spending more on the military than on education and health care, and keeping itself in power by razing the countries' natural resources and pocketing the profits, would qualify as 'least favored'.

Ideally, one should hope that the prospect of favorable trade relations with GFP countries would stimulate the governments of non-GFP countries to adopt policies in line with sustainable development. Mostly, though, this hope would prove idle. Especially in poor, non-democratically governed countries the political and economic leadership would consider GFN programs as a frontal attack on their privileges. They would therefore do their utmost to block the coming to power of a GFP government. The obstacles would be greatest in totalitarian states, where government control of the media would make it difficult for the GFN and GFP to get their message across and gain public support. Elsewhere, deliberate misinformation of the public, vote rigging and the intimidation of candidates as well as voters could be used to prevent a GFP from coming to power.

Outside pressure could help break the hold of governments engaging in such practices over their nations. Cut-backs in trade and aid could lead to dissatisfaction among the politically influential salary and business groups. That could create a climate in which support for alternative movements like the GFN-GFP could grow. In extreme cases, pressure for change could also be generated more directly, through consumer boycotts and government embargoes. However, these weapons should be used only after very careful consideration, particularly with regard to negative consequences for the population. In deciding whether to engage in a boycott, the GFN and GFP from the country involved would have to have a decisive say.

Besides putting pressure on national governments, GFNs and GFPs should also aim to push international institutions towards policies in line with sustainable development. Especially the IMF and World Bank should be pressured into taking a longer term perspective on development. Structural adjustment programs should no longer focus exclusively on reducing government expenditure and generating foreign exchange for debt servicing. Rather, IMF and World Bank should promote policies aimed at the development of people and the rational use of natural resources. Since the early 1990s, they've already made a modest beginning with this. Unfortunately, though, they still finance programs to foster such policies with loans—thus worsening the debt problem even further. If the past holds any lessons, this means that as in the nations involved debt loads increase, further cutbacks in social and environmental programs can be expected.

IMF and World Bank could contribute to sustainable development by providing loans only for economically viable projects, while helping nations to obtain grant aid for social en environmental programs. Loans and other assistance should be given only to countries that would take all the necessary steps for sustainable development: provision of good quality education and health care for all layers of the population, fostering the sustainable use of land and water, creating well-functioning public institutions, and developing a sound tax system in which the rich would pay their dues. Considering the huge influence of IMF and World Bank on poor nations' economic, fiscal and development policies, they could well become a very effective instrument for change.

Why a new organization?

Why it is necessary to create the GFN-GFP movement in a world already flooded with organizations striving for sustainable development? Why not, instead, bring together existing organizations, in a kind of forum that could do the same as the GFN?

There would be several problems with this approach. One is the very fact that the number of organizations focusing on sustainable development issues is so huge. Each works in its particular field, following its specific strategy and interests. Although there is a lot of cooperation, there is also competition, especially with regard to funding. And though many such organizations have comparable objectives, visions on how these should be achieved vary greatly. To bring all these organizations together physically would already be an enormous and costly task; to bring them to agree on joint goals and strategy would be practically impossible. Even if it could be done, the financial cost and amount of time involved would be huge. Such funds and time would be better spent, by both the GFN and other organizations, in pursuing their specific goals.

Then, there is the problem of politics. Many organizations, especially those focusing on a single issue (for example, the environment, health care, or alleviating poverty), refrain from taking political standpoints, so as to be able to work with governments of different political backgrounds. The GFN, as this book makes clear, would have no such reservations. It would not only translate the measures required for sustainable development into a coherent, political program, but also, compare the latter with programs of existing political parties. Although the need for this is easily argued, the standpoint of many organizations that taking political standpoints would compromise their work is equally justifiable. Getting such organizations to join a forum with clear political overtones would be difficult if not impossible. Therefore, it would be preferable to create a looser relationship.

The above implies that, instead of trying to have existing organizations join forces, it would be better to form a new one. The GFN would be unique in that it would cover all areas relevant for worldwide sustainable development in a coherent way. It would draw up an integrated set of plans for sustainable development, starting at the global level and descending to the regional, national, and local levels. Thanks to the many governmental and non-governmental organizations that already work on issues related to sustainable development, many of the building blocks of those plans are already available. What would remain for the GFN would be to fill in the gaps, and to incorporate all building blocks into a coherent design.

As implied above, the GFN would also be complementary to existing organizations in the political sense. To carry out sustainable development programs would require genuine international cooperation and coordination. That is unlikely to come off the ground as long as politicians keep using conflictive engagement to defend their own and their constituencies' short term interests. With the support of the many organizations already involved in sustainable development, the GFN could start to pressure the political establishment to change its attitudes and policies. Where such pressure would fail to do the job the GFP, by converting the GFNs mobilizing force into direct political power, would come to renew the political establishment.

Local and global initiatives

Growing numbers of people and organizations see globalization and the resulting concentration of economic and political power, especially in multinational corporations and international financial markets, as a serious threat to society.[1] Their answer is decentralization: to strengthen economic and political power at the local level. The Financial Micro-Initiatives discussed in Chapter XIII were one example, but there are many more: even at the World Bank decentralization (albeit only political) has become a hot issue.

How does the GFN-GFP concept fit in this perspective? At first sight there appears to be a problem: the GFN, with its goal of developing and implementing a global development plan, appears to call for centralization rather than decentralization. That, however, would be a misinterpretation. As indicated earlier in the Chapter, GFN programs would not be blueprints for rigid central planning, but policy frameworks that would leave plenty of room for local decision making. On the other hand, even those most eager to return power to the community will have to admit that current trends cannot be countered by small scale initiatives only. A countervailing power is needed at the national and international level: an organization that can take on the centers of power and the ruling dogma that economic globalization and the nation state's loss of control over economic processes is as inevitable as it is beneficial. To do so a clear, coherent alternative is needed, and an international power base that can create the conditions and context for political and economic decentralization. The goal of the GFN would be to provide this alternative and, in tandem with the GFP, to form that power base.

In conclusion, there would be complementarity between, on the one hand, the GFN-GFP and on the other, groups aiming for sustainable, locally based development. The same would be true with regard to organizations targeting specific issues such as the environment, poverty or human rights. The GFN and later, GFP would need the expertise and grass roots support of single issue and community organizations to create and implement a framework for sustainable development. Vice versa, these organizations would need a GFN and a GFP to create and implement a national and international policy framework in line with their goals. Thus, close cooperation between GFN-GFP, single issue organizations and local community initiatives would be an essential step on the road to sustainable development.

Conclusions

'Never doubt that a small group of thoughtful, committed citizens can change the world. Indeed, it's the only thing that ever has.'

Margaret Mead, Anthropologist

Chapter XIV

CONCLUSIONS

The need for sustainable development

The goal of sustainable development is to have all human beings, including future generations, live their lives in health and freedom, with access to everything that's needed to fully develop their physical and mental potential. To achieve this, a number of problems must be overcome. Let's review them briefly.

At present, society is moving away from rather than closer to sustainable development. In the rich countries, more and more people enter the ranks of the poor. Lower and middle income groups work harder and produce more, but don't get rewarded for it. Due to the cost cutting efforts of business and government, everyone faces growing economic insecurity: jobs that are here today may be gone tomorrow.

In the poor countries, one third of the population—one fifth of humanity —is so desperately poor that life is a day-to-day struggle for survival. A group at least as big lives just above that level. Their number increases daily, mostly due to rapid population growth.

Basic conditions for escaping poverty are health and education. World-wide, the poor and the lower income groups depend on governments to provide these. Yet due to the efforts to cut budget deficits, debts and the role of government, the quality of and access to such services is reduced. Consequently, the living standards of billions of people are in decline, and their chances to better themselves diminished.

In the future, the problem of declining living standards is likely to be worsened by environmental degradation. Today, environmental problems already affect the health and livelihoods of hundreds of millions, especially in the poor countries. If drastic steps are not taken, in the coming century billions will suffer the consequences of pollution and scarcity of natural resources—including agricultural land and water.

Current economic developments and policies contribute to the above processes. The worldwide opening up of economies has led to cut-throat competition in the marketplace. Technological development, fueled by the need to cut production costs, leads to rapid productivity growth. At the same time, demand stagnates due to rising unemployment, declining real wages and cutbacks in government investment. The economy is caught in a vicious circle, marked by a growing gap between productivity and demand. We're going towards a situation in which the demand for goods and services can be supplied with only a fraction of the labor available in the world today. That means that, from an economic point of view, a large part of the global work force is or will soon become superfluous.

The problem of development, therefore, is more social than economic. The solution is not, as economists and most politicians claim, to maximize economic growth by meeting demand in the most efficient way. Rather, it is to generate development that enables all people to make a decent living, in ways that guarantee that future generations can do the same.

The starting point for giving people, all people, the chance to partake successfully in the economy is to make good quality education and health care available to all. Second, especially in the poor countries and the impoverished parts of the rich nations, huge investments will have to be made in social and economic infrastructure. Simultaneously, to ensure acceptable living conditions for future generations, we need to rationalize our use of finite natural resources. To do so, we have to control pollution, make adequate use of land and water, and convert to renewable energy. Again, vast investments are needed.

Unfortunately, present economic dogma and policies obstruct these investments. The key problem is that the above needs are not backed up by economic demand, that is, the capacity to pay. Without this capacity, the productive potential of the private sector cannot be used to supply the required goods and services. It is the State which, as guardian of the common good, should assume the responsibility to satisfy people's basic needs when they're incapable of doing so themselves. Yet bad government, resulting in the misspending of funds and towering debts, has led to a drive to reduce the role of the State in society as much as possible. Consequently, its capacity to invest in sustainable development is declining rather than growing.

Whereas the lower-income groups face increasing poverty and economic stagnation, the top layers of society are appropriating ever more of its wealth. This accumulation of capital leads to large scale speculation. Unavoidably, this will be followed, at some point in time, by a financial and economic collapse. Those hardest hit will be, as usual, the less well-off. Moreover, the State's capacity to invest in sustainable development will be reduced even further.

The key to resolving these problems is to convert the needs of humanity into demand. The only institution that can do so is the State. If it does it in the right way, it can create economic growth that is both socially equitable and environmentally sustainable. We've seen how part of the money needed for sustainable development can be raised by reversing some of the flows of riches that go to the wealthy. Higher taxes on high incomes, on capital transactions and on capital gains would be one option. Reducing the possibilities for tax avoidance, coming down hard on tax evasion, and the confiscation of any illegally obtained wealth, property and profits should be complementary measures.

Sustainable development should also be financed through the taxation of non-sustainable economic activities, including the use of non-renewable energy. Government bureaucracies should be downsized; moreover, in most countries the armed forces should be abolished. Different ways of budgeting and the elimination of subsidies that funnel support to those who don't need it would also generate huge savings and thus, more funding for sustainable development.

The above measures would yield hundreds of billions of dollars each year. The cost of a full program for sustainable development would, however, require even more funds. These should be raised through conditioned money creation. This would be possible without causing inflation, as long as total demand for goods and services would not exceed the global economy's production capacity.

If adequately handled, money creation would lead not only to sustained economic growth, but also bridge the growing gap between productivity and demand. Moreover, it would put an end to today's addiction to deficit financing and could wean private investors from the international speculative circuit, by offering them new investment opportunities.

The measures proposed in this book require a radical change in economic and political thought. This change will not be easy, because the short term interests of many of today's political and economic power holders will suffer. Yet even for them, the alternative presented in this book would, in the longer run, be beneficial.

The strongest argument for gaining support for sustainable development is its importance for future generations. People are concerned not only about their own well-being, but also about that of their offspring. Even for the rich this should provide an incentive to try and do something about the problems we face. For this incentive to work, however, it is necessary that people become aware of the problems. For those who already support the idea of sustainable development, the challenge is to raise this awareness with others.

People should come to realize that we're all in this together: that the main problems we face are of a global nature. Economic and environmental problems as well as most social and political issues can only be solved through international cooperation. Futurist Marshall McLuhan coined the phrase 'global village' to indicate that with modern technology, people all over the world will be able to communicate as easily as if they were neighbors. His prophecy has already come true. Yet how many people will get citizenship in this global village and gain access to all its amenities? The question is not a lack of production capacity: in principle, in a few decades, everyone could be hooked up to the international communication network. The problem is that people lack the money to convert their need into demand. As things are going, McLuhan's vision will involve only a privileged minority—of millions, not of billions.

The concept of a global village demonstrates that the need for sustainable development is worldwide: that we're all in this together. To extend the 'village' metaphor, we can see the world's regions as extended families—fathers and mothers, aunts and uncles, sisters, brothers and cousins, all living together in compounds. A few of these extended families are rich, with most family members leading a life in various degrees of luxury. Some are relatively poor: although they don't starve, they are unable to afford many of the things their better-off family members have come to take for granted.

For the other extended families, who make up the majority of the village, poverty is much more pervasive and acute. More than half the members, including most of the children, live in deprivation; some are actually on the brink of starvation. Many children do not go to school or receive medical care because ostensibly, the family lacks the money to pay for it. Yet the heads of these families live in an opulence which in some cases, surpasses that of the rich members of the rich families.

Part of this opulence comes from loans that the heads of the rich families gave to those of the poor. This money was supposed to be spent to improve the poor families' compounds. But the heads of the poor families pocketed most of it, thus enriching themselves. Still the loans have to be paid back—with interest. The money to do so comes not out of the well-filled pockets of the family heads, but from the overall budgets of the poor families. Conse-quently, the poorest family members have even less food and money than be-fore. The kids can't go to school; when someone falls ill, there's no money for the doctor. The house is in a shambles, piping and wiring are derelict or wrecked. Children fall ill and die. Only the part of the house where the fami-ly heads live is in good shape. Having all the amenities, they're not affected by, and appear to have little interest in, the worsening conditions in the rest of the compound.

Assume that we are members of one of the few rich families. What would we do in such a situation? We'd help the poor family members to at least send the children to school and, in case they'd fall ill, to pay for the doctor. Also, we might assist them in getting clean water, cleaning up their garbage and fixing their sewers, so their kids wouldn't fall ill so easily. That would not be totally altruistic, as the stench of their waste sometimes bothers us. We might even lend the poor neighbors some money to help them set up a small business.

All this would not really cost us a whole lot—say, 1 or 2% of our income. We could do it without eating a calorie less. We might have to cut down on a few luxury items and we might buy our new car a year later.

Why would we feel this urge to help? We would feel a moral obligation, strengthened by the fact that our family would be partly to blame for the poor families' predicament. In particular, we would feel guilty about our neighbors having to suffer for not paying off a loan which they didn't borrow and from which they never saw any benefits.

More parallels can be drawn. Assume that our destitute neighbors have a grove of trees in their farmyard, with a brook that provides both them and us with water. Since we razed our trees a long time ago, theirs are also important to us. Unfortunately, out of sheer need they are rapidly cutting them down, as the wood is one of the few things they can sell for a reasonable price. We know that the trees are essential for the entire neighborhood—yet some of our family are in fact the biggest buyers of the wood and thus promote the trees' destruction.

Moreover, assume that because of their poverty and lack of opportunity, some poor neighbors are regularly at our door to ask for work. As they become increasingly destitute, they come over more and more often. They even try to get in without asking. It's getting so bad we're thinking of fencing ourselves in completely.

On the other hand, if we can help them protect their trees and plant some new ones, we're all better off. If we help them raise their incomes they'll come to a store we own to buy the products we sell. That way, we'll also be better off.

Unfortunately, those who run our financial affairs claim there is not enough money to help our poverty ridden neighbors—we can't even help their kids. And to a certain extent, they're right. After all, all of us are on top of them if they reduce our household's budget and say we'll have to wait another year for a new car.

So much for analogies. The point is that for the better-off in our world, the fight against poverty and environmental degradation has two imperatives. One is self-interest: if they don't, they'll suffer the consequences as well. The other is moral: as human beings, we have a responsibility to help others who are in need—especially if we, or at least those who represent us, are partly responsible for their misery. Both imperatives call for people to broaden their perspective: from their family, ethnic group, their region and nation, to humanity as a whole. Technology has made it possible for us to become aware of events all over the world, and to communicate with each other, worldwide, in a matter of seconds. Now, technological progress should be paired with moral progress. The rich should be willing to contribute some of their wealth for investment for the benefit of all. Moreover, those less well-off should be supported, materially as well as politically, in their struggle against those who exploit, repress or, in the best of cases, ignore them. The ruling cliques who do so have in many instances been created and supported by the democratically chosen leaders of the rich nations. Both the former and the latter should be held accountable by voters and made to change their policies.

Investment in worldwide sustainable development will require some sacrifice, but the benefits will be huge. Politicians should focus on convincing the public of the need to make those investments. Conversely, voters must require their leaders to end the parochial defending of short term interests, to correct past mistakes and to start addressing the real needs of society.

Denial

Denial of the problems we face is a major obstacle to change. Such denial is particularly prevalent among a small but highly visible group of opinion leaders and politicians who have a strong influence on public opinion. Politicians tend to downplay society's problems—unless they can gain votes by blaming problems on the opposition. That is because voters like to hear optimism: the idea that a beautiful future lies ahead, and the promise that such a future can be attained by voting for the right candidate. Since politicians need votes they may, to a certain extent, be excused for saying what their constituencies want to hear.

There is, however, no reason why other opinion leaders should deny society's problems. Yet many economists, columnists, journalists and other pundits keep on telling us that things are going well, except for a few glitches which will sort themselves out. This playing down of current problems and even more, of the dangers that lie ahead, is a prime cause of the failure to take effective action. Supported by mainstream economic thought, which claims free trade, a tight money supply, deregulation and balanced budgets will resolve all economic problems, it becomes the most formidable obstacle to investment for sustainable development.

This obstacle must, and can be overcome. Awareness of the problems, concern for one's offspring and empathy for those who are less well-off should motivate those who can afford it to push for investment in sustainable development. Tangible proof that such investment yields results will increase the willingness to contribute. On the other hand, the longer we wait with investing, the more difficult and costly it will be to remedy the problems we face.

Starting up the process

We're at a crossroads. The present holders of political and economic power, supported by most of the middle class, can stick to the present path. They can continue to seize and consume an ever larger part of the world's resources, while environmental degradation and poverty increase. Alternatively, the well-off can choose, or be forced, to change present policies and invest in sustainable development.

Starting the process of sustainable development requires a joint effort of citizenry and leadership. In normal times, such a collective effort is difficult to generate, particularly in a democracy. The different groups and individuals that make up society pursue their own agendas, which may or may not conflict with those of others. In special situations, however, it is possible to focus these energies into a single, unified force. For this to happen the leadership and a sizeable majority of the population must strongly agree on the need to achieve a clearly defined goal. Also, they should have a clear idea of how that goal should be attained. This was the case, for example, for the allied democracies that fought World War II. The goal was the destruction of national socialism and fascism. The strategy was war for total victory. Especially in Europe and Japan, such a common purpose could also be observed in the two decades after the war. The goal was reconstruction; the means, hard work.

In such situations, visionary leaders can inspire the population to make huge sacrifices for the common good. The war effort was one example, but so was, for the U.S., the Marshall Plan. Through this plan, more than $100 billion (in today's dollars) was generated to help Western Europe and Japan back on their feet. Correctly, U.S. leaders saw this as an investment that would more than pay itself back—as indeed it did: Western Europe and Japan developed into wealthy new markets, providing a huge boost to the US economy. Moreover, the Marshall Plan helped put the countries involved firmly in the democratic camp, making them strong U.S. allies.

The vision and capability required to create programs such as the Marshall Plan, and generate the public support needed to carry them out, are sorely lacking today. Up till now, our leaders have been unable to formulate a clear goal, much less a clear strategy for development. For reasons explained in this book, it is highly unlikely that current leaders and politicians will be able to unite and set in motion a process of genuine sustainable development. Even less likely is that they can inspire the public to make the needed sacrifices. Instead, as members of the privileged minority that has enriched itself at the cost of the rest of society, they are likely to avoid the topic of sacrifice altogether.

Today's political establishment, then, is unlikely to reform itself. Among the public, however, the potential to push for change is greater than ever. Since the early 1990's, voters have been looking for new leadership. Both in the newly emerged democracies and in countries with a longer democratic tradition, including most of the rich nations, many people are fed up with politics as usual. They get tired of politicians who, rather then address society's problems, spend their time pandering to special interests and quarreling with political opponents. Thus considered, the outlook for a movement as described in Chapter XIII is better than ever.

There is yet another circumstance favoring change: people have faster access to more information. Thanks to the rapid evolvement of mass communication and the increased freedom of information that has accompanied democratization, the possibilities of spreading new ideas are better than ever. Even so, radical ideas for change such as those proposed in this book are unlikely to gain momentum. It is even less likely that a movement to put those ideas into practice would actually get off the ground and take on the proportions needed to achieve significant and lasting change. But that's no reason not to try. Many major events in world history were set in motion in even less favorable circumstances, and came about against greater odds.

Perhaps the best reason for hope is that the huge benefits of sustainable development can be obtained at minimal cost. The solutions and strategies suggested in this book would require sacrifices only from a small, rich minority. Even they would not see a significant decline in their standard of living, much less be deprived of the basic necessities of life. On the other hand, almost everybody, including those members of the rich and powerful who earn their wealth in respectable ways, would come out on top. Not only in terms of better health, improved physical and economic security, and a cleaner and safer environment, but also as a result of the economic opportunities created by sustainable development.

The limits to growth

One of the points made in this book is that investment in sustainable development would create strong economic growth. Today, that would mean increased consumption of finite natural resources. Even if production is transformed in the ways suggested in this book, non-renewable resources will still be used. And even when measures to limit pollution to an absolute minimum are all carried out, continuing growth will mean that the carrying capacity of the world's ecosystem will, at some point, be exceeded.

It is therefore obvious that we should strive for a balanced, no-growth situation at some point in the future. This will come about as people realize that a further increase in production and wealth is no longer called for. As productivity increases, people can choose to have more leisure instead of higher incomes, and spend more time on activities that do not consume finite resources. Rising productivity resulting from technological development could then be used not to create more wealth, but to decrease work time. Thus, when the primary goal of sustainable development is achieved, the aim should become to arrive at a state of ecological, social and economic equilibrium.

This equilibrium would never be perfect. Even with the most advanced forms of recycling, no production cycle can be 100% efficient: there will always be losses of non-renewable raw materials, especially metals. Therefore, at some point in the future the need will arise to look outside our planet for new raw materials. That could make space exploration and, in the far future, the mining of other planets a condition for maintaining the living standards that by then, people will have become accustomed to. The effort this would require could provide humanity with a new, collective, greater purpose.

Such a purpose is important not only in a material, but also in a psychological sense. People need a greater, common purpose, going beyond personal interests, to achieve the form of collective well-being and optimism that makes life gratifying. In Europe and the u.s., this common purpose existed in the post-war decades—a time remembered by most of those who lived through it as one of happiness and optimism. Today, that greater purpose should be sustainable development; in the future, it could be the conquest of space.

Involvement, critique and flexibility

So what next? You, the reader, may agree that the problems discussed in this book are real and need solving. You may also agree that our current leadership is unlikely to start up the process of change. You may even feel that the approach offered in this book could make a difference. Even so, chances are you'll put this book aside—and that's that.

For setting us on the path to sustainable development, that won't do. On the other hand, it will not be necessary to mount the barricades either. Many people contributing a little can create the snowball effect that is needed. Point out books like this to people who might be interested. Discuss themes related to sustainable development when the opportunity presents itself. Support organizations involved in one or more of the components of sustainable development. Perhaps, some day, join a movement as proposed in this book.

Most important of all is to maintain an attitude of constructive criticism. A prime condition for sustainable development is the awareness that to get ahead, people must unite. They must overcome differences and compromise where necessary. Take this book as an example. Few readers will agree with all the analyses, solutions and strategies proposed. Environmentalists may challenge a strategy that involves growth even for the rich countries, arguing that for a rational use of natural resources, the latter must shrink their economies. Proponents of small scale initiatives for development will denounce the proposed large scale approach based on a global development plan. Nationalists from poor countries are likely to condemn the conditioning of aid and the role attributed to transnational business. Market buffs may join small-scalers in criticizing the key role attributed to the state. Conservatives are sure to find fault with this also, as well as with the emphasis put on the rehabilitation of offenders. On the other hand, liberals are likely to decry the suggestions aimed at keeping unrepentant offenders from the streets.

My first response to such opinions is that everything in this book is open for discussion. Reasonable argument can lead to new conclusions and better ideas for solutions. But if you have objections, don't wait until all of them are overcome. Instead, look at the tenet of sustainable development in general—and judge if what is proposed offers a better perspective than what is currently done and advocated. When the conclusion is that in spite of all its shortcomings, the things proposed in this book go in the right direction, offer support.

As I've indicated, one of the basic operating principles of a movement for sustainable development should be that every analysis and proposal is open for discussion. If alternative solutions and strategies can be argued to be more effective, they should replace or supplement what has already been proposed. Reason, unbiased analysis and flexibility, not dogma, should be the intellectual basis for sustainable development. Yet this openness should not lead to endless discussions on every theme related to sustainable development. Mechanisms should be used to limit such debates to an exposition of views and analysis of arguments, followed by a clear-cut decision on the course to be followed. In exceptional cases of continuing disagreement, arbitration could provide the answer. Then, all involved would have to be flexible enough to abide by the outcome, even if it were contrary to their original point of view.

Mass and individual support

A basic condition for sustainable development is mass support. The biggest challenge of all is to generate that support among a public that is already numbed by an endless flow of information. To break through this numbness, it is crucial to gain the support of at least part of society's opinion leaders: of the members of our intellectual, cultural, political and economic elites. Obtaining this support will be difficult. People will have to discard ways of thought that are so deeply ingrained that they've become dogmas. What's worse, those who *can* muster the intellectual flexibility to do so will expose themselves to the ridicule of colleagues who cannot. And of course, if any-

212 ❖   GLOBAL DEVELOPMENT: PROBLEMS, SOLUTIONS, STRATEGY

thing approaching what has been proposed in this book is set in motion, members of the present political and economic elites would stand to lose some of their power and wealth. Still, there is hope. In all elites, there are members who dare to go against the grain, have a strong social conscience and are aware of the dangers we face if we continue on the current path. They should be drawn aboard to give the movement momentum.

Another group of key importance, but difficult to recruit, is the scientific community. In an era of increasing academic specialization, scholars expose themselves to ridicule when actively engaging in efforts to change society. Scientists as well as journalists are held to a professional code of 'objectivity', which keeps them from identifying with calls for action.

Yet here also there is reason for hope. In late 1992 more than 1600 scientists, including 102 Nobel laureates, collectively signed a 'Warning to Humanity'. It states the following: 'No more than a few decades remain before the chance to avert the threats we now confront will be lost and the prospects for humanity immeasurably diminished. A new ethic is required—a new attitude towards discharging our responsibility for caring for ourselves and for the earth. This ethic must motivate a great movement, convincing governments and reluctant peoples to effect the needed changes'.

Unfortunately, such initiatives do not receive the attention they merit. If the movement proposed by the 1600 has come about, only few people know about it. In the media, the *laissez faire* point of view continues to prevail: mainstream economists and conservative opinion leaders still swamp the natural and social scientists who emphasize the need to address environmental degradation and poverty.

The challenge, then, is to start the 'great movement' the 'Warning to Humanity' proposes. The backing of key opinion leaders could help such a movement to muster mass support. In the final instance, however, the key to meaningful change lies with the individual. *You* can make a difference. In pondering if you will do so, there is one thing you should remember: doing nothing would *not* imply remaining neutral. On the contrary, it would amount to support for the *status quo*, and thus, for the continuing abuse of our natural resources and for policies that are liable to perpetuate and in the longer run, increase poverty and human suffering. On the other hand, supporting the drive for sustainable development would imply backing an effort to provide economic and physical security for all people, and to make the earth a habitable place for future generations—including your own offspring. The choice is yours.

EPILOGUE: WHAT NEXT?

Global Development sets forth the main obstacles to sustainable development, proposes solutions, and suggests the formation of an organization to get those solutions implemented. At the time of the book's first printing, no such organization existed. If it is formed depends on the response *Global Development* generates, which means it depends on you, the reader. Write to indicate your interest in remaining informed of future developments and possibly, in joining and becoming active in a to-be-formed Global Future Network. Of course, any additional comments or suggestions, on the formation of such a Network or on other issues discussed in this book, are also very welcome.

An organization will need working capital. In time, therefore, you may receive a request for an initial monetary contribution, to cover the costs of staying in touch with you, to set up an administration, and especially, to bring this book to the attention of a wider audience. To the latter, you can already contribute by pointing out or perhaps, giving this book to family, friends and acquaintances. Any suggestions you may have for fund raising, from people, foundations and other organizations that espouse principles in line with sustainable development, would also be greatly appreciated. If enough money can be raised, staff could be contracted to start drawing up the global development program and, where initial response to the book is greatest, national programs. By then, the momentum gained should be sufficient to initiate the other GFN activities described in Chapter XIII.

There are a lot of *if*'s in the above. With your support, they can be overcome. Get in touch, preferably by e-mail, to *gfn@freemail.nl*. If you do not have access to e-mail please write to the author at the following address: Oudlaan 13, 6708 RC Wageningen, The Netherlands. It could help set in motion a movement with the potential to change our world for the better.

NOTES

Chapter I

1 *The Economist*, June 11, 1994.
2 OECD *Employment Outlook 1997*, press release of July 10 1997, obtained from the Internet, http://www.oecd.org.
3 *Newsweek*, June 23, 1997.
4 *Newsweek*, February 27, 1995.
5 *Time*, October 24, 1994, citing data of the U.S. Bureau of the Census.
6 Estimates given by economist Lester Thurow in an article in *New York Times Magazine*, which appeared in translation in *de Volkskrant* of December 2, 1995.
7 Newsweek, October 3, 1994.
8 Estimate in *de Volkskrant*, January 6, 1996.
9 Data from *de Volkskrant*, June 17, 1995. The expansion of the economy is calculated on the basis of an average annual growth rate of 2.6% over the 10-year period.
10 *The Economist*, April 30, 1994, citing from Paul Krugman's book *Peddling Prosperity*.
11 *The Economist*, July 30, 1994.

Chapter II

1 Data presented in the 1992 Labor Party election manifesto.
2 Food and Agricultural Organization (FAO) and World Health Organization (WHO), 1992. *Nutrition and development: a global assessment*. Rome, Italy.
3 World Bank, 1992. *World Development Report 1992: Development and the Environment*. Oxford University Press, New York.
4 Overview of the *Human Development Report 1997*, published on the Internet, http://www.undp. org, accessed on July 11, 1997.
5 Overview of the *Human Development Report 1997*, on the Internet.
6 Lester R. Brown et al., 1994. *State of the World 1993: A Worldwatch Institute Report on Progress Towards a Sustainable Society*. W.W. Norton & Company, New York.
7 UNDP, *1992 World Development Report*, op.cit.

8 Overview of the UNDP *Human Development Report 1997*, presented on the Internet, http://www. undp.org, July 1997.

9 Lester R. Brown et al., *State of the World 1993*, op.cit.

10 Cited in *Newsweek*, February 13, 1995.

11 For a host of telling examples of the poor actually suffering from aid projects and programs, see a.o. Graham Hancock, *Lords of Poverty*. Macmillan London, 1989 / Mandarin Paperbacks, London 1991, and more recently, Bruce Rich, *Mortgaging the Earth: The World Bank, Environmental Impoverishment, and the Crisis of Development*, Beacon Press, Boston, 1994.

12 According to data from the European Network on Debt and Development, cited in *de Volkskrant* of Monday, October 3, 1994.

13 Cited in the *Volkskrant* of January 23, 1995.

14 *Global Development Finance Extracts*, 1997, from the Internet, http://www. worldbank.org, July 1997.

15 According to the 1994 Human Development Report of the United Nations, cited in *Newsweek*, August 1, 1994.

16 Estimate by former Nigerian military strongman Olusegun Obasanjo, the first military leader in Nigeria to abandon power voluntarily, made during a conference on African leadership in Uganda held in December 1994. Reported in *de Volkskrant*, December 14, 1994.

17 *de Volkskrant*, December 28, 1994.

18 Estimate by economist John Kenneth Galbraith, at a conference on the Economics of Safety held in Holland in 1993.

19 UNDP data cited by Paul Harrison, 1993. *Inside the Third World: the anatomy of poverty*. Penguin Books, London.

20 *The Economist*, May 7, 1994.

21 The United Nations Development Program, cited in the Worldwatch Institute's 1995 *State of the World* Report, estimates that overall, only 7% of total bilateral aid (direct aid between countries) and 16% of multilateral aid funds (aid channeled via international organizations) goes to programs for primary education, health care, family planning and sanitation.

22 Quoted in *The Economist*, May 7th, 1994.

Chapter III

1 Source: *de Volkskrant*, February 15, 1992, in an interview with a leading American diplomat involved in negotiations for the World Climate Treaty. This treaty was to be signed at the United Nations Conference on Environment and Development (UNCED), held in Rio de Janeiro in June 1992.

2 *Newsweek*, June 1, 1992.

3 Quoted in *Newsweek*, December 12, 1994.

4 Cited by the Worldwatch Institute in its 1993 *State of the World* report, op.cit.

5 World Bank, *1992 World Development Report*, quoted in *de Volkskrant*, May 18, 1992.

6 Meadows, Donella H., Dennis L. Meadows and Jorgen Randers, 1992. *Beyond the limits. Confronting global collapse; envisioning a sustainable future.* Earthscan Publications, Ltd., London-Chelsea Green.

7 Brown, L.R., et al. *State of the World 1994*, op.cit.

8 Goldsmith, E., and N. Hildyard, 1990. *The Earth Report 2: Monitoring the battle for our environment.* Mitchell Beazley, London.

9 Meadows et al., *Beyond the Limits*, op.cit.

10 Paul Harrison, *Inside the Third World*, op.cit.

11 Data on health costs and lost productivity are from *The Health Costs of Air Pollution* by James S. Cannon, published by the American Lung Association in 1985. Data on agriculture are from a joint study of the U.S. Environmental Protection Agency and the U.S. Department of Agriculture. Both studies are quoted in the 1993 *State of the World* report, op.cit.

12 Data cited in *Beyond the limits*, op.cit.

13 Lester Brown et al. *1994 State of the World Report*. World Watch Institute, Washington DC.

14 *de Volkskrant*, September 24, 1997.

15 Goldsmith & Hildyard, *The Earth Report 2*, op.cit.

16 Brown et al., 1993 *State of the World* report, op.cit.

17 Data from The United Nations Environment Program (UNEP) and the International Soil Reference and Information Center in Wageningen, the Netherlands.

18 Brown et al., 1994 *State of the World* report, op.cit.

19 Goldsmith & Hildyard, *The Earth Report 2*, op.cit.

20 Brown et al., 1993 *State of the World* report, op.cit.

21 Goldsmith & Hildyard, *The Earth Report 2*, op.cit.

22 Brown et al., 1993 *State of the World* report, op.cit.

23 U.N. estimates, cited by the 1993 *State of the World* report, op.cit.

24 World Commission on Environment and Development, 1987. *Food 2000: Global policies for sustainable agriculture.* Zed books, London/New Jersey.

25 *The Earth Report 2*, op.cit., and the 1993 *State of the World* report, op.cit.

26 Goldsmith & Hildyard, *The Earth Report 2*, op.cit.

27 Meadows et al., *Beyond the Limits*, op.cit.

28 Data from *Beyond the Limits*, op.cit.

29 *State of the World 1994*, op.cit.

30 *State of the World 1993*, op.cit.

31 For a more detailed description of this issue see Richard Douthwaite, *Short circuit: Strengthening Local Economies for security in an Unstable World*, The Lilliput Press, Dublin, Ireland, 1996.

32 *The Economist*, May 23, 1992.

Chapter IV

1 *Newsweek*, August 15, 1994.
2 *de Volkskrant*, December 17, 1991, citing data collected by the management consulting firm McKinsey.
3 *Newsweek*, August 15, 1994.
4 *de Volkskrant*, June 9, 1995.
5 Estimate by David Bickford of Inter Access risk Management, cited in *de Volkskrant*, February 15, 1997.
6 The difference between indirect and white collar crime as defined here is that whereas the former makes no direct victims, white collar crime can very well be aimed at individuals—as is the case with swindling and fraud. In practice, though, most white collar crime is indirect, as a result of which the two terms can almost be used interchangeably.
7 Data from Canadian criminologist Irvin Waller of the University of Ottawa, presented in his inaugural address to a United Nations conference on crime prevention, held in Paris in 1992.
8 Data from Canadian criminologist Irvin Waller, op.cit.
9 Data from Canadian criminologist Irvin Waller, op.cit.

Chapter VI

1 *The Economist*, June 27, 1992.
2 See for detailed descriptions of and arguments for local development Richard Douthwaite's *Short circuit: Strengthening Local Economies for security in an Unstable World*, The Lilliput Press, Dublin, 1996, and David C. Korten's *When corporations rule the world*, Earthscan publications, London, 1995.

Chapter VIII

1 Data from *Beyond the Limits*, op.cit.
2 As is argued in, among others, *Beyond the Limits*, op.cit.
3 *Beyond the Limits*, op.cit.
4 Worldwatch Institute, *State of the World 1991*, op.cit.
5 University of Utrecht, 1994. *Growing with less energy*. Utrecht, Holland.
6 Studies cited in *de Volkskrant*, November 10, 1992.
7 Worldwatch Institute, 1992. *Empowering Development, The New Energy Equation*. Washington DC, U.S.
8 Worldwatch Institute, *State of the World 1991, 1992, 1995*, op.cit.
9 Worldwatch Institute, *State of the World 1994*, op.cit.
10 Worldwatch Institute, *State of the World 1994*, op.cit.
11 Quoted in *The Earth Report 2*, op.cit.
12 For more details and various examples of CSAs see Richard Douthwaite's *Short cir-*

cuit: Strengthening Local Economies for security in an Unstable World, The Lilliput Press, Dublin, 1996.
13 Estimates of the Australian Bureau of Agricultural and Resource Economics, on the basis of EC information.
14 *The Economist*, June 27, 1992.

Chapter XI

1 Worldwatch Institute, *State of the World 1993*, op.cit.
2 Data from an interview with John Cregan, president of the US Business and Industrial Organization (a business lobby group in Washington), in *de Volkskrant*, April 25, 1992.
3 *The Economist*, April 30, 1994, citing from Paul Krugman's book "Peddling Prosperity".
4 Data from *The culture of contentment*, 1992, by John Kenneth Galbraith, op.cit.
5 *de Volkskrant*, April 26, 1997.
6 Data from the U.S. Census Bureau, presented on the Internet, http://www.census.gov, July 1997.
7 Calculations based on data from the U.S. Census Bureau, presented on the Internet, op.cit.
8 Worldwatch Institute, *State of the World 1995*, op.cit.

Chapter XII

1 *The Economist*, October 8, 1994.
2 For example, *de Volkskrant* of January 19, 1995 reported that in December 1994, with the U.S. economy in full swing, 85.4% of production capacity was used. That was the highest figure since October 1979.
3 For a detailed description of the FMI concept and examples of how it works in practice see Richard Douthwaite's 1996 book *Short circuit: Strengthening Local Economies for security in an Unstable World*, The Lilliput Press, Dublin, Ireland.
4 See for examples Douthwaite 1996, op cit., and the report *Balancing Europe for sustainability: Using financial micro-initiatives to build a better environment*, Aktie Strohalm, Oudegracht 42, 3511 AR Utrecht, The Netherlands.

Chapter XIII

1 See, among others, David C. Korten's *When corporations rule the world*, Earthscan publications, London, 1995, and Richard Douthwaite's *Short circuit: Strengthening Local Economies for security in an Unstable world*, op.cit.

INDEX